Planning for Two Transformations in Education and Learning Technology

Report of a Workshop

Committee on Improving Learning with
Information Technology

Roy Pea, Wm. A. Wulf, Stuart W. Elliott, and
Martha A. Darling, Editors

Center for Education and Board on Behavioral,
Cognitive, and Sensory Sciences
Division of Behavioral and Social Sciences and Education

Computer Science and Telecommunications Board
Division on Engineering and Physical Sciences

NATIONAL RESEARCH COUNCIL
OF THE NATIONAL ACADEMIES

THE NATIONAL ACADEMIES PRESS
Washington, D.C.
www.nap.edu

THE NATIONAL ACADEMIES PRESS   500 Fifth Street N.W.   Washington, DC 20001

NOTICE: The project that is the subject of this report was approved by the Governing Board of the National Research Council, whose members are drawn from the councils of the National Academy of Sciences, the National Academy of Engineering, and the Institute of Medicine. The members of the committee responsible for the report were chosen for their special competences and with regard for appropriate balance.

This study was supported by Contract/Grant No. R303U000001 between the National Academy of Sciences and the U.S. Department of Education. Any opinions, findings, conclusions, or recommendations expressed in this publication are those of the author(s) and do not necessarily reflect the views of the organizations or agencies that provided support for the project.

Library of Congress Cataloging-in-Publication Data

Planning for two transformations in education and learning technology : report of a workshop / Committee on Improving Learning with Information Technology ; Roy Pea ... [et al.] editors.
   p. cm.
"Center for Education and Board on Behavioral, Cognitive, and Sensory Sciences, Division of Behavioral and Social Sciences and Education. Computer Science and Telecommunications Board, Division on Engineering and Physical Sciences." Includes bibliographical references.
  ISBN 0-309-08954-9 (pbk.) -- ISBN 0-309-51940-3 (PDF)
  1. Education--United States--Data processing--Congresses. 2. Information technology--United States--Congresses. 3. Education--Effect of technological innovations on--United States--Congresses. I. Pea, Roy D. II. National Research Council (U.S.). Committee on Improving Learning with Information Technology.
LB1028.43.P59 2003
371.33'4--dc21
                          2003012605

Additional copies of this report are available from National Academies Press, 500 Fifth Street, N.W., Lockbox 285, Washington, DC 20055; (800) 624-6242 or (202) 334-3313 (in the Washington metropolitan area); Internet, http://www.nap.edu

Printed in the United States of America
Copyright 2003 by the National Academy of Sciences. All rights reserved.

Suggested citation: National Research Council. (2003). *Planning for Two Transformations in Education and Learning Technology: Report of a Workshop.* Committee on Improving Learning with Information Technology. R. Pea, Wm. A. Wulf, S.W. Elliott, and M.A. Darling (Eds). Center for Education and Board on Behavioral, Cognitive, and Sensory Sciences, Division of Behavioral and Social Sciences and Education and Computer Science and Telecommunications Board, Division on Engineering and Physical Sciences. Washington, DC: The National Academies Press.

THE NATIONAL ACADEMIES
Advisers to the Nation on Science, Engineering, and Medicine

The **National Academy of Sciences** is a private, nonprofit, self-perpetuating society of distinguished scholars engaged in scientific and engineering research, dedicated to the furtherance of science and technology and to their use for the general welfare. Upon the authority of the charter granted to it by the Congress in 1863, the Academy has a mandate that requires it to advise the federal government on scientific and technical matters. Dr. Bruce M. Alberts is president of the National Academy of Sciences.

The **National Academy of Engineering** was established in 1964, under the charter of the National Academy of Sciences, as a parallel organization of outstanding engineers. It is autonomous in its administration and in the selection of its members, sharing with the National Academy of Sciences the responsibility for advising the federal government. The National Academy of Engineering also sponsors engineering programs aimed at meeting national needs, encourages education and research, and recognizes the superior achievements of engineers. Dr. Wm. A. Wulf is president of the National Academy of Engineering.

The **Institute of Medicine** was established in 1970 by the National Academy of Sciences to secure the services of eminent members of appropriate professions in the examination of policy matters pertaining to the health of the public. The Institute acts under the responsibility given to the National Academy of Sciences by its congressional charter to be an adviser to the federal government and, upon its own initiative, to identify issues of medical care, research, and education. Dr. Harvey V. Fineberg is president of the Institute of Medicine.

The **National Research Council** was organized by the National Academy of Sciences in 1916 to associate the broad community of science and technology with the Academy's purposes of furthering knowledge and advising the federal government. Functioning in accordance with general policies determined by the Academy, the Council has become the principal operating agency of both the National Academy of Sciences and the National Academy of Engineering in providing services to the government, the public, and the scientific and engineering communities. The Council is administered jointly by both Academies and the Institute of Medicine. Dr. Bruce M. Alberts and Dr. Wm. A. Wulf are chair and vice chair, respectively, of the National Research Council.

www.national-academies.org

COMMITTEE ON IMPROVING LEARNING WITH INFORMATION TECHNOLOGY

ROY PEA *(Cochair)*, School of Education, Stanford University
WM. A. WULF *(Cochair)*, National Academy of Engineering, Washington, DC
BARBARA ALLEN, Project LemonLINK, Lemon Grove, CA
EDWARD R. DIETERLE II, Harvard Graduate School of Education
DAVID DWYER, Apex Learning, Bellevue, WA
LOUIS M. GOMEZ, School of Education and Social Policy, Northwestern University
AMY JO KIM, There, Menlo Park, CA
EDWARD D. LAZOWSKA, Department of Computer Science and Engineering, University of Washington
MIRIAM MASULLO, New Canaan, CT
JAMES W. PELLEGRINO, Department of Psychology, University of Illinois-Chicago
LOUIS PUGLIESE, onCourse, Washington, DC
MARSHALL S. SMITH, William and Flora Hewlett Foundation, Menlo Park, CA
DAVID VOGT, New Media Innovation Center, Vancouver, BC
BARBARA WATKINS, Chicago Public Schools
LINDA S. WILSON, International SEMATECH, Austin, TX

MARTHA A. DARLING, *Special Consultant*
KEVIN AYLESWORTH, *Study Director,* Center for Education (until September 2002)
STUART W. ELLIOTT, *Study Director*
JAY B. LABOV, *Deputy Director*
GAIL PRITCHARD, *Program Officer* (until March 2002)
DOUG SPRUNGER, *Program Associate*
TINA WINTERS, *Research Assistant*
TERRY HOLMER, *Senior Project Assistant*
CHRISTINE R. HARTEL *Director,* Board on Behavioral, Cognitive, and Sensory Sciences
TIMOTHY READY, *Program Officer*
HERBERT S. LIN, *Senior Scientist,* Division on Engineering and Physical Sciences

Acknowledgments

The Committee on Improving Learning with Information Technology (ILIT) would like to thank the many people who made our work possible. Our sponsor, the U.S. Department of Education, provided generous support to the project. Numerous presenters and participants at the project's January 2001 workshop (see National Research Council [NRC], 2002b) shared their insights about the use of information technology to improve learning and the nature of the committee's task. The participants in the December 2001 and January 2003 workshops (listed in Appendix C) provided stimulating conversation that is reflected throughout this report and greatly contributed to the work of the committee. At the December 2001 workshop, thought-provoking presentations were made by Tom Landauer, University of Colorado; Marlene Scardamalia and Chris Teplovs, University of Toronto; Susan Goldman, University of Illinois at Chicago; Bernard Dodge, San Diego State University; Randy Hinrichs, Microsoft Research Lab; Joseph Krajcik, University of Michigan; Doug Kirkpatrick and Marcia Linn, University of California at Berkeley; and Eliot Soloway, University of Michigan. In addition, there were numerous people involved in technology demonstrations for Knowledge Forum, Little Planet Literacy Series, WebQuest, Web-based Inquiry Science Environment (WISE), Science Laboratory of the Center for Highly Interactive Computing (hi-ce), and probeware for the iPaq. In conjunction with the workshop, the committee conducted site visits at Adobe,

Scientific Learning, New Tech High School, Apple Computer, and Sun Microsystems, which included discussions with many people at those organizations. At the January 2003 workshop, in addition to a number of presentations by members of the committee, there were insightful discussions by Darryl LaGace, Lemon Grove School District in California; Steve Rappaport, Advanced Networks and Services; Cheryl Lemke, Metiri Group; Wanda Bussey, Rufus King High School; Geneva Henry, Rice University; Robert Tinker, Concord Consortium; Nora Sabelli, SRI International; Milton Goldberg, National Alliance of Business; and Terry Rogers, Advanced Network and Services.

At the NRC, the committee would like to thank Kevin Aylesworth, who was study director until September 2002, for his able guidance of this project. Upon Kevin's departure, Stuart Elliott stepped into the position and helped the committee complete its work. Jay Labov, deputy director of the Center for Education (CFE), provided general oversight throughout the project. Martha Darling, special consultant, provided extensive assistance in planning and carrying out the January 2003 workshop and helping draft this summary report. Herbert Lin, senior scientist at the Computer Science and Telecommunications Board in the Division on Engineering and Physical Sciences and Christine Hartel, staff director, and Timothy Ready, program officer, both of the Board on Behavioral, Cognitive and Sensory Sciences in the Division of Behavioral and Social Sciences and Education, provided additional guidance and perspective from their respective communities. Terry Holmer, CFE senior project assistant, provided critical logistical coordination of the workshop and committee meetings. Gail Pritchard, CFE program officer, Doug Sprunger, CFE program associate, and Tina Winters, CFE research assistant, provided important research and organizational support during the evolution of the committee's work.

This report has been reviewed in draft form by individuals chosen for their diverse perspectives and technical expertise, in accordance with procedures approved by the Report Review Committee of the NRC. The purpose of this independent review is to provide candid and critical comments that will assist the institution in making its published report as sound as possible and to ensure that the report meets institutional standards for objectivity, evidence, and responsiveness to the charge. The review comments and draft manuscript remain confidential to protect the integrity of the process. We thank the following individuals for their review of this report: Stephen C. Ehrmann, The Teaching, Learning, and Technology Group, Takoma Park, MD; John Jungck, Beloit College, Beloit, WI; Nora Sabelli, Center for Technology and Learning, SRI International, Menlo Park, CA; Lee S. Sproull, Stern School of Management, New York

ACKNOWLEDGMENTS

University; Ronald Stevens, University of California, Los Angeles; and James Yao, College Station, TX.

Although the reviewers listed above provided many constructive comments and suggestions, they were not asked to endorse the content of the report nor did they see the final draft of the report before its release. The review of this report was overseen by Nicholas J. Turro, Columbia University. Appointed by the NRC, he was responsible for making certain that an independent examination of this report was carried out in accordance with institutional procedures and that all review comments were carefully considered. Responsibility for the final content of this report rests entirely with the authoring committee and the institution.

Contents

1	**INTRODUCTION**	1
	Origins and Purpose of the Project	1
	Challenges and Grounds for Optimism	2
	Approach to the Task	5
	Issues and Themes	7
	Organization of the Report	10
2	**PRELIMINARY COMMUNITY BUILDING AND ROADMAPPING EFFORTS**	11
	January 2001 Workshop and the Decision to Use Roadmapping	11
	Rationale for Roadmapping	13
	December 2001 Workshop	15
	The Committee's Experience with Roadmapping After the December 2001 Workshop	16
	Analytical Challenges	20
	Preliminary Roadmapping Goal Tables	22
	Annex to Chapter	23
3	**JANUARY 2003 WORKSHOP**	35
	First Transformation	35
	Key Enablers for the First Transformation	51
	Second Transformation	52
	Key Enablers for the Second Transformation	66
	Next Steps for the National Academies	67

REFERENCES		72
APPENDIXES		
A	Reflections and Next Steps	79
	Putting High-Quality Content on the Web Available Free to All *Louis Pugliese and Marshall S. Smith*	79
	A Pull Learning Paradigm *David Vogt*	81
	A Vision for LENS Centers: Learning Expeditions in Networked Systems for 21st Century Learning *Roy Pea and Edward Lazowska*	84
	Reasons for Optimism, Possibilities for Hardware and Software *Edward Lazowska and Roy Pea*	90
	Reflections on Teaching and Teachers in the LemonLINK Environment *Barbara Allen*	91
	The Potential for Collaboration Already Exists Within the Educational Community Fabric *Linda S. Wilson*	96
	Improving Learning with Information Technology *Edward R. Dieterle II*	100
	Developing, Deploying, and Evaluating High-Quality Software for Teaching English to English Language Learner Students and for Tutoring and Providing Practice in Reading and Mathematics for Students Who Need Extra Support *Marshall S. Smith*	103
	Changes in Technology and Its Application to Learning *Miriam Masullo*	105
	Technology and the Advancement of Educational Assessment *James W. Pellegrino*	107
B	Key Enablers for the Two Transformations	113
C	Workshop Materials	117
D	Biographical Sketches of Committee Members	128

1

Introduction

ORIGINS AND PURPOSE OF THE PROJECT

This project grew out of ongoing concern by the U.S. Department of Education, education practitioners, education researchers, and members of the information technology[1] community that the potential of information technology (IT) to transform K-12 education for all remains unrealized. While many pioneering IT projects have been developed by the education research community and individual schools or school districts and examples of commercially and publicly available IT for supporting language arts, mathematics, science, and technology education abound, there is a growing recognition that IT hardware and applications are having less influence on improving learning for all than has been envisioned. Despite the frustration about the unrealized potential, however, there is a sense of optimism that the motivation to confront and address the issue is gaining momentum. What may be needed most are mechanisms and incentives for the IT, education research, and practitioner communities to share their challenges and collective wisdom, to work together in strategic and sustained ways, and to focus on quality improvement of products and services for the benefit of all students. The purpose of this project was to explore opportunities for moving these communities in this direction.

---

[1] A diverse group spans this category, including producers of hardware, software, and services used in education, with industry sectors as diverse as publishers, computing, telecommunications, cable, and television.

CHALLENGES AND GROUNDS FOR OPTIMISM

With the many innovations and applications of information technologies developed for supporting learning and teaching in the past decade, these technologies may finally be able to play transformational roles in enabling learning to higher standards (e.g., Means et al., 1993; President's Committee of Advisors on Science and Technology (PCAST), 1997; President's Information Technology Advisory Committee (PITAC), 1999, 2001; Pea et al., 1999; Roschelle et al., 2001; Web-Based Education Commission, 2000), in individualizing instruction to all learners (National Research Council, 2001b), and in fostering continual teacher professional development (e.g., National Commission on Mathematics and Science Teaching for the 21st Century, 2000; Goldman, 2001). These innovations and applications of IT include web-based, hyperlinked, multimedia, interactive 2-D and 3-D graphics and animations, modeling, data visualization, geolocation, and community-oriented features. Currently, the United States possesses an infrastructure in which over three-quarters of all classrooms have Internet access and multiple computers for student use (Cattagni and Farris, 2001). This change is due to the billions of dollars that American schools have expended in the past five years on the costs of information technology and telecommunications, with funding enabled by the E-Rate (discounted telecommunications services for schools and libraries) and other federal programs, as well as state and local initiatives.

The expectations are not to "replace" teachers with technologies that students use entirely on their own, as earlier critics of computer-assisted instruction and integrated learning systems feared, nor to naively assume that uses of computers will translate automatically into cost efficiencies and gains in achievement test scores. Umbrage is rightly directed at such "silver bullet" thinking, because education systems, like business systems, are far too complex for adoptions of specific interventions to translate into predictable outcomes. After a decade of sustained research on what has come to be called "systemic reform" (Smith and O'Day, 1991), it is obvious that there are tremendous variations in how any specific educational intervention is implemented. Such differences are not surprising, given the enormous amount of variability in local education systems and how their components interact.

Success in implementing educational interventions is especially dependent on the capacities of teachers to provide high-quality instruction with these new approaches (e.g., Boesel, 2001; Darling-Hammond and Sykes, 1999; *Education Week*, 2000; Haycock, 1998; National Commission on Teaching and America's Future [NCTAF], 1996). Theory and research that examine systemic reform recognize the intricate interplay among these education system components—including student characteristics and classroom groupings, curriculum, classroom tasks and assessments, teacher proficiencies and professional development opportunities, school leadership, and community involvement—and at different levels, from the classroom, to the school, to the district, state, and federal levels (e.g., Goetz et al., 1996). The decentralized nature of education in the United States adds to this mix the special caprices of local decision making and different standards for what students should know and be able to do across states and locales.

Despite these complexities in implementation and the difficulties they pose for understanding the impact of education technology on learning and student achievement, current research shows that the impact of IT can be substantial. This is the case even though one might expect that the more significant impacts of technology on teaching and learning will accumulate only slowly over time. In meta-analytic studies that examine effect sizes aggregated across many different studies, relationships between various educational interventions and student achievement have been demonstrated, including those of computer-assisted instruction (e.g., Hattie et al., 1996). In a recent comprehensive review of hundreds of studies conducted since 1994 on the effectiveness of "discrete educational software"[2] for K-12 learning achievements, Murphy et al. (2002, p. 2) concluded that "the research base is severely limited" since "out of the 195 experimental or quasi-experimental evaluation studies that our initial search identified, just 31 studies used designs that met our minimum requirement for methodological criteria: the use of a comparison group, large enough samples, reliable measures of achievement, and sufficient information for estimating an effect size." Nonetheless, with these stringent criteria secured, their meta-analysis did support a positive association between the use of discrete educational software products and student achievement in reading and mathematics, with an overall weighted effect size of +0.38 standard deviation.[3,4] This effect size is consistent with and slightly larger than earlier meta-analyses of computer-based instruction. For comparison, the authors note that "many educators believe

---

[2] As contrasted with more open-ended uses of computers as tools for such purposes as writing, creating presentations, spreadsheet models, or web-based project research. "Discrete educational software" includes not only integrated learning systems and computer-assisted instruction but also CD-ROM and Internet-based learning programs, such as Knowledge Adventure's *Math Blaster* and Renaissance Learning's *Accelerated Reader* (Murphy et al., 2002).

[3] The metric of "effect size" standardizes the difference between a treatment and control group by dividing that difference by the standard deviation of the performance in the control group. Murphy et al. (2002) used a "weighted effect size" as a more reliable estimate of the effect of use of educational software on achievement, as the reliability of the estimated effect for a given study increases with its sample size.

[4] A similar conclusion is reported in another recent meta-analysis of the effects of technology on student outcomes (Waxman et al., 2002).

reducing class size is an effective way to improve learning, but effect sizes for studies of class size reduction are between +0.13 and +0.18" (p. 35).

Many new paradigms for IT use diverge from the discrete educational programs that have dominated technology in education over the first 20 years that microcomputers have been employed in K-12 settings and that have been the subject of existing meta-analyses. Those previously dominant technologies (e.g., computer-assisted instruction and integrated learning systems) target skill training in core subject areas, such as reading and mathematics. They employ methods such as drill and practice, skill games, exercises, memory games, review and reinforcement tutorials, and problem-solving simulations (e.g., Foshay, 2000). The new paradigms of IT use cover a broader range of applications. As characterized by the report, *How People Learn* (National Research Council, 2000), there are five classes of use for information technologies in K-12 education that are grounded in the learning sciences:

1. Supporting learning in real-world contexts, such as with inquiry projects that allow students to collect scientific data in the natural environment.

2. Connecting learners to experts and communities of other learners.

3. Providing scaffolds and tools to enhance learning, such as visualization and analysis tools that enable students to utilize complex data for higher order thinking.

4. Providing opportunities for feedback, reflection, and revision in the acquisition and construction of knowledge, such as with intelligent tutoring systems.

5. Expanding opportunities for teacher learning, using methods such as on-line communities of practice and best-practice case studies.

The types of IT application described in *How People Learn* have great potential for improving teacher learning and professionalization, for connecting learners via telecommunications to the distributed expertise of others from whom they can learn, for using student responses much more frequently in formative assessments that can guide instructional practices, and for providing far broader student access to complex concepts and skills more typically associated with only advanced learners by using visualization and other dynamic knowledge representation techniques (e.g., National Research Council, 2000; Kaput, Noss, and Hoyles, 2001; Pea, 2002; Linn, Davis, and Bell, 2003). As many of these more recent developments and applications using IT in K-12 learning engage multiple aspects of systemic reform, from curriculum to assessment to teacher development and parental involvement, they may offer great potential to have impacts on learning that go well beyond those demonstrated for discrete educational programs in the meta-analytic reviews cited above (e.g., National Research Council, 2000; Roschelle et al., 2001).

APPROACH TO THE TASK

In response to concerns about the continued unrealized potential of IT in K-12 education, the National Research Council's Division of Behavioral and Social Sciences and Education, Center for Education (CFE), Board on Behavioral, Cognitive, and Sensory Sciences (BBCSS), and Computer Science and Telecommunications Board (CSTB) undertook a collaborative project to help the IT, education research, and practitioner communities work together to find ways of improving the use of IT in K-12 education for the benefit of all students. The project was supported by the U.S. Department of Education. Its purpose was to catalyze the creation of a community of experts in technology, cognition and learning, and education who are devoted to improving education through creative and research-based development and applications of information technology. This project examined a range of work in the field, from creating innovations, to research that tests whether specific innovations are able to improve learning and teaching, to the implementation steps needed to make those resources and techniques available to all teachers and students.

The committee conducted its work according to the following statement of task: "This project is a collaborative activity of the Division of Behavioral and Social Sciences and Education, the Center for Education (CFE), the Board on Behavioral, Cognitive, and Sensory Sciences (BBCSS), and the Computer Science and Telecommunications Board (CSTB) to catalyze the creation of a community of experts in technology, cognition and learning, and education who are devoted to improving education through creative and research-based applications of information technology."

While the primary focus of this project has been at the K-12 level, there are clear cross-cutting issues and opportunities for intersections with higher education (e.g., National Research Council, 1997, 1999a, 2002a, 2002c) and the workplace (National Research Council, 1998, 2001a).

The project was conducted in two phases. In the first phase, the project's statement of task called for a steering committee to hold a workshop in January 2001 to make an initial roadmap of core issues and explore the potential for new applications of computing in schools, colleges, and universities. That workshop also featured lessons learned from successful partnerships that have productively engaged educators, researchers in the learning sciences, and industry in powerful models of using IT to improve learning and teaching. A report on this workshop was issued in 2002 (National Research Council, 2002b).

In the second phase, the steering committee was augmented with additional experts in the field of cognition and learning, education practice, information technology, community building, and the technique of roadmapping. For this second phase, the project's statement of task called for the committee to help develop the roadmapping process, to help build a community of experts devoted to improving education through creative and research-based applications of information technology, and to plan future activities in this area.

The enlarged committee held a meeting in summer 2001 to explore the issues surrounding the building of a professional community concerned about ways to develop, market, and utilize IT to improve K-12 education. The committee then conducted a workshop in December 2001 to build additional ties to the larger community of stakeholders and to further develop the roadmapping process. The results of this road-mapping exercise suggested two primary themes, which the committee describes below as "transformations":

1. integrating cheap, fast, robust computers into instruction for every student in the United States, and

2. combining advances in the science of learning with IT capabilities to dramatically improve student learning.

The first transformation deals with the infrastructure that will be required to integrate IT into education for all students. This infrastructure is construed broadly to include not only the *development and support* of hardware and software by the IT industry, but also *ongoing professional development* for teachers to assist them in implementing classroom use of technology, *equitable access* to software that can fundamentally change the ways that teachers and other educators think about and develop curriculum, and *mechanisms for providing students and parents ready access* to such resources outside the school environment.

The second transformation deals with the research and development efforts that will be required to mine the scientific literature on how people learn and apply it to all aspects of the development, implementation, and professional development that will be part of the next generation of educational and learning technologies. As suggested by a number of reports (e.g., National Research Council 1997, 2000, 2001b), this next generation of technology could improve learning by such means as supporting deeper conceptual learning and providing more useful, individualized formative assessment to guide instruction.

The committee met again in June 2002 for intense work on the roadmapping process. In January 2003 the committee convened a final workshop involving the larger community of stakeholders to explore in greater depth the two transformations that had emerged from its preliminary roadmapping. This workshop included a discussion of the types of activities that would be useful to pursue to advance the appropriate and effective use of IT to improve K-12 teaching and learning. This report describes the outcome of the January 2003 workshop, along with an overview of the work that preceded it.

The goal of the committee has been to work toward bringing together insights and findings concerning effective conditions for learning and teaching with IT in the learning sciences, the pioneering work of innovative educators, and the developments of learning technologies provided by the industrial sector, including hardware, software, publishing, service and professional development supports. The committee's efforts in this regard can help to foster a community across the sectors of learning sciences research, education, and industry to articulate and achieve a vision for strategically improving learning with information technologies. Such a community would work to monitor developments in technology, learning research, and classroom practice to help inform local district decisions about how to use education technology, governmental decisions about the research agenda and financial support in education technology, industry decisions about how to supply the market for education technology, and researcher decisions about how to design studies that address the pressing questions, challenges, and opportunities faced by today's educators with respect to information technology (e.g., National Research Council, 1999a, 2001a).

ISSUES AND THEMES

Despite the promise and demonstrated success of information technology, the effective use of IT in education continues to fall far short of what is possible in improving education for all learners. The committee's work uncovered a number of requirements for IT to be broadly applied to improve learning. These requirements emerged as recurrent themes in the committee's workshop discussions and roadmapping exercises. The later sections of this report provide more detail about those discussions and exercises; the following list is a guide to them:

1. The importance of focusing the use of IT on improving the teaching and learning of academic skills, content, and higher order thinking rather than on learning how to use the technology.

2. The importance of providing a one-to-one student:computer ratio to enable IT to be fully integrated into teaching and learning.[5]

---

[5] A one-to-one student:computer ratio is not in conflict with the goal of group learning. Indeed, with on-line sharing tools, a one-to-one ratio is likely to enhance group learning in education in many of the same ways that it can enhance group productivity in the workplace. However, additional research is needed to evaluate this conjecture. Such one-to-one computing also enables new kinds of classroom communications for embedded assessments, in which all students respond to questions posed by the teacher and students' responses are statistically aggregated and displayed as a reflection for the class and the teacher of what the students understand or find problematic (e.g., Roschelle and Pea, 2002).

3. The importance of providing reliable and easy-to-use IT that both maximizes the time students can spend using the technology to learn and minimizes the support cost to keep that technology operational.

4. The importance of teachers understanding the benefits of fully integrating IT into their work compared with current approaches and tools in the classroom. The most important benefits from embracing the new technologies would be improved student learning and superior work flow management—from standards-based lesson planning and media use, to implementing and supporting student learning activity customized to needs, to assessment and next-step responsive teaching.

5. The importance of providing easy ways for teachers to locate appropriate software for IT that provides high-quality learning and teaching experiences.

6. The importance of addressing the disconnect in the educational hardware and software markets between the products currently developed and offered by industry and the kind of products that teachers could use effectively to improve student learning. As technology continues to develop, it may become practical and appropriate to develop IT hardware specifically targeted to the needs of the education market.

7. The importance of addressing IT-related change with systemic approaches that better align and integrate curriculum, instruction and assessment, and appropriate teacher development.

8. The importance of investigating the possible use of hardware and software developed for consumer markets, such as cell phones and gaming systems, for supporting learning and education applications as well.

9. The importance of exploiting the significant and still unrealized opportunity to employ emerging evidence from the learning sciences to improve the effectiveness of IT applications.

10. The importance of defining and investing in long-term research to develop and test new approaches for improving student learning with IT that can be replicated and adapted for use by many student audiences. It is also important to bring them to a scale of use that would benefit students and educators in many more educational environments than happens traditionally by means of government-sponsored research activities.

The January 2003 workshop resulted in a number of suggestions for key enablers of the two transformations in the use of information technology to improve learning. These suggestions are listed in Box 1-1 and are discussed in more detail in Chapter 3. The workshop also included a discussion of the next steps the National Academies might take to help bring about the two transformations. The categories of suggestions are listed in Box 1-2 and are presented in more detail in Chapter 3.

BOX 1-1 Key Enablers

**The First Transformation:
Integrating Cheap, Fast, Robust Computers into Instruction for
Every Student in the United States**

- Demonstrating the value of technology for student achievement and teacher work practices.
- Taking a systems approach to the integration of technology, encompassing curriculum, pedagogy, assessment, and technical support.
- Embedding technology in teacher pre-service and in-service education.

**The Second Transformation:
Combining Advances in the Science of Learning with
IT Capabilities to Dramatically Improve Student Learning**

- Defining research and development goals for improving learning with technology, including identification of desired targets coupled with intermediate milestones that can make improvement visible.
- Supporting large-scale and long-term research and development efforts ranging from proof-of-concept test beds to partnerships in IT parks.
- Developing new approaches to assessments that are capable of measuring such 21st century skills as visual literacy and complexity management (see Chapter 3).
- Creating a better functioning market for education technology by fostering broad communications and collaboration between supplier-developers and actual K-12 practitioner-users.

BOX 1-2 Next Steps for the National Academies

- Assessing effective IT tools and uses and raising awareness of those with potential for improving learning.
- Identifying policies that promote and hinder effective use of IT.
- Defining a research agenda for use of technology in K-12 education.
- Identifying research designs for testing IT applications that are appropriate to different types of research questions.
- Investigating market failures in education technology with a view to facilitating new understandings between industry and K-12 education about their respective needs.
- Applying research on organizational change to K-12 education in order to close the gap between the development of innovative approaches to improve learning and their broad implementation.

ORGANIZATION OF THE REPORT

Following this introduction, Chapter 2 provides background information about the committee's workshops that occurred in January 2001 and December 2001 and about the committee's experience using the technique of roadmapping as a tool for strategic thinking and planning. Chapter 3 is a detailed summary of the discussion that occurred at the January 2003 workshop. Appendix A consists of personal statements by committee members regarding next steps to encourage the effective use of IT in K-12 education. Appendix B provides the complete set of key enablers for the two transformations that were developed by the breakout groups in the January 2003 workshop. Appendix C provides the agenda and the participant list for the December 2001 and the January 2003 workshops. Appendix D provides biographical sketches of the committee members.

2

Preliminary Community Building and Roadmapping Efforts

JANUARY 2001 WORKSHOP AND THE DECISION TO USE ROADMAPPING

In spring 2000, representatives from the U.S. Department of Education (DoEd) and senior staff at the National Academies had identified two common frustrations. First, the innovations, resources, and strategic planning that have been devoted to developing information technologies that are transforming American and global business practices have been much less focused on the comparable opportunities for transforming education. Second, research in the cognitive and learning sciences—which has elucidated important principles of human learning with major implications and potential for improving education (e.g., National Research Council, 2000, 2001b)—has not been fully utilized in the design, implementation, and evaluation of technology tools that could enhance learning to an even greater degree.

Based on the critical need to find ways for the interests of these communities to converge toward the improvement of learning for K-12 students, the National Research Council and the U.S. Department of Education decided to launch a project to bridge communication among the technology, education research, and education practitioner communities. The mandates given to the committee for this project include finding ways to meld expertise among individuals in three domains:

- experts in the cognitive and learning sciences who have explored the practical uses of IT in education;

- practitioners in the education community who understand the opportunities and the challenges for improving teaching in U.S. schools; and
- those in the IT sector who are committed to improving education, including those from the hardware sector who wish to adapt their commercial equipment to better meet the financial and technological constraints of the K-12 community and software developers who can design new tools and applications for use primarily in education.

Three goals were identified:

- to establish ongoing dialogue and interactions among the technology, learning and cognition, and education practitioner communities for the purpose of improving education for all learners through the development and appropriate uses of modern technology;
- to find ways to incorporate the knowledge base, research findings, and innovations from each of these communities into coherent strategic approaches to developing education technologies; and
- to offer information so that the end users of education technologies can make better informed decisions about the purchase, use, and maintenance of these technologies and, in addition, can develop the capacity to offer the kinds of professional development programs that will enable teachers to use education technologies in ways that can transform teaching and learning.

To accomplish these goals, the committee organized a large workshop that was held at the National Academy of Sciences building in Washington, DC, in January 2001. People from all three communities were invited to attend and discuss how to forge an extended community of expertise from the three domains. They also were asked to explore how, by working together, strategic decisions could be made about how IT products could be developed based on evidence from the cognitive and learning sciences about ways to enhance learning and teaching. Finally, in plenary and breakout sessions, participants considered how education practitioners could both use this expanded knowledge base and contribute to the strategic design of IT product development as well as the direction of education research that focuses on the use of IT.

Descriptions of presentations about various models of IT use in schools that seem to be improving learning, the rich conversations that surrounded those presentations, the innovative ideas that many participants contributed to this workshop in both plenary and breakout sessions, and possible next steps for the committee to undertake are detailed in a separate report (National Research Council, 2002b). At the meeting of the committee following the workshop, it quickly became clear that a model of action would be required to continue and expand the dialogue among these communities and to help them set both individual and collective goals in the near and longer term for improving learning and teaching with IT. The model for accomplishing this work that quickly surfaced was to use the process of roadmapping, which had been employed by the semiconductor, automotive, and other industries. All of these industries faced similar dilemmas: bringing together representatives from organizations with different, often competing kinds of expertise, needs, and goals, to focus their attention on solving issues that would benefit all sectors of those expanded communities.

Several members of the committee had had direct experience with the roadmapping process and were able to help the committee envision a roadmap that would guide its future activities and serve as way to encourage others in the IT, research, and practitioner communities, to engage in similar kinds of work for their mutual benefit and, most importantly, for the benefit of the nation's schoolchildren. The next section describes the process in some detail.

RATIONALE FOR ROADMAPPING

Roadmapping is a tool for showing the structural and temporal relationships that are embedded in the task of achieving a particular set of goals (e.g., Kostoff and Schaller, 2001; Phaal, Farrukh, and Probert, 2001). In the words of Robert Galvin, who led Motorola during its use of the technique, roadmapping is an "inventory of possibilities for a given field" (Schaller, 1999). The structural relationships may involve interim products, experiments, techniques, insights, and policy changes. Temporal relationships may be related to developmental or product cycles, time to build a facility, and time to learn and use new knowledge and skills. These elements help establish areas in which additional research is needed to advance the system of interest toward the specified goals. They also help determine whether the research need is shorter or longer term. Thus they can generate the core of a research agenda for the issue being roadmapped.

The process can also offer a powerful tool for organizing discussions. By showing how disparate tasks link to common goals, roadmapping can bring competing groups and contrary views into a focused discussion. Furthermore, it can be a way to coordinate efforts across different disciplines and sectors and across many levels—local, state, national, international—toward one or more stated goals. Among the benefits of roadmapping are that it helps identify connections between parts of the problem that may not at first inspection appear to be directly related, and it can show the relationships between the desired goals and the high-risk tasks that are embedded in the problem. Done right, roadmapping is inclusive, and many stakeholders can tune their efforts (grants, research programs, development budgets, product planning, etc.) to it. One of the primary potential problems with roadmapping is that often no external standards exist that could help define goals, provide guidance on how to reach those goals, or indicate that they have been achieved. Moreover, people can sometimes interpret the goals too literally, which can stifle innovative solutions.

There are encouraging examples of the use of roadmapping in a number of other fields, a situation that at a general level suggests that the technique may be useful in education as well (Kostoff and Schaller, 2001; Phaal, Farrukh, and Probert, 2001; Schaller, 1999). These examples include roadmapping efforts focused on an industry sector (Semiconductor Industry Association), on products (Motorola, Phillips), on product/technology (Lucent/Wireless) and on cross-boundary issues (Department of Energy). For example, the latter has employed roadmapping in its work on a variety of complex cross-boundary issues. According to the Department of Energy (2000), roadmapping is "most valuable" when any of the following is present:

- high potential for mission failure;
- significant consequences if failure occurs;
- high dollar costs, high worker exposure, or high environmental impact;
- multiple, diverse efforts working on a common problem; and
- significant political or senior management visibility.

Like many of the needs of K-12 education, improving learning with information technology appeared to meet all five criteria described in the Department of Energy roadmapping process.

In applying roadmapping to the issue of improving learning with information technology, the committee sought to deal with two of the challenges it was asked to address: (1) the complexity along many dimensions, including technical, economic, behavioral, and political aspects, of using IT to improve K-12 learning and teaching, and (2) the need to bring together three quite different and disconnected constituencies at the outset even to begin the conversation, with broader engagement required later in the process. Complexity and the need for community building have been important features of previous efforts in other sectors of the economy that have turned to roadmapping as a strategic planning technique.

The committee's charge anticipated that the project would offer an opportunity to build a community of interest among the three groups:

researchers in the learning sciences, K-12 practitioners, and IT developers. The concept of inclusiveness is central to roadmapping, as great benefits flow from the full expression of diverse views and perspectives in goal-focused discussions. As the committee's roadmapping effort matured, engagement of a broader group of stakeholders was envisioned, including parents, school boards, teacher unions, K-12 administrators, schools of education, university learning scientists, IT companies, business leaders, and policy makers. Certainly, as many have learned over the last two decades of attempts to improve education and expand educational opportunities to all students, effecting any change in highly decentralized education systems requires the participation of a wide array of actors whose interests may be in competition or may work at cross-purposes to each other.

DECEMBER 2001 WORKSHOP

In conjunction with its third meeting in December 2001, the committee organized and sponsored a second workshop. That workshop, held in Palo Alto, California, featured presentations and targeted plenary and breakout discussions that were designed to assist the committee with its work of articulating a roadmap for improving learning with information technology.

Following the first workshop, committee members and staff recognized the enormous breadth of issues that could be associated with this work. As a result, a decision was made to narrow the focus of this second workshop to feature advances in the uses of IT in the areas of reading and middle school science. Because discussions at the first symposium focused on such a broad array of topics, the second symposium focused more specifically on the uses of IT in the areas of reading and middle school science. However, these topics did not prove to provide a meaningful focus for the committee's subsequent roadmapping exercises; committee members came to realize that what is applicable to this subject area could apply equally well to many other subjects. Of course, different software is often needed to use IT effectively in different subject areas of the curriculum. However, the broad systemic issues that must be addressed to ensure that IT is used effectively to improve learning do not vary substantially across different subject areas, and the committee elected to conduct its roadmapping exercise around more universal and generic issues.

The second workshop provided opportunities to bring together additional representatives and voices from the larger community that has dedicated itself to improving learning with information technology. In addition to presentations, the workshop also featured a series of demonstrations of products that are currently being used and are undergoing various kinds of evaluation to measure their efficacy for improving reading or middle school science. The workshop ended with breakout groups that discussed how the demonstrated technologies could be used to address needs in these subject areas. The agenda for the workshop and the list of participants appear in Appendix C.

THE COMMITTEE'S EXPERIENCE WITH ROADMAPPING AFTER THE DECEMBER 2001 WORKSHOP

The committee launched the roadmapping effort at a meeting that followed the December 2001 workshop. Guided loosely by the sequence of steps identified in the roadmapping literature, the committee: (1) began with an initial set of participants representing learning scientists, K-12 educators, and IT developers (the committee members themselves), but with plans to share its preliminary work with a more inclusive group of stakeholders and to incorporate their multiple perspectives; (2) agreed on boundary conditions, originally with the intention to focus on the opportunities and challenges to improve middle school science education; (3) sought to identify both shorter and longer term goals that could lead to significant improvements in learning and teaching through the strategic use of IT; and (4) created an initial roadmap based on the desired goals.

During the course of 2002, the committee encountered a number of challenges in terms of both process and its analytical charge. The process challenges are summarized here, and the analytical challenges of improving learning with information technology are addressed in the following section.

The Roadmapping Challenge

Although the committee set out along the lines suggested by the roadmapping literature, the very nature of the National Research Council committee process, in which committee members are volunteers who serve pro bono, meant that our efforts would differ from the full roadmapping efforts found in other sectors. Typically, roadmapping entails an intense commitment of time, resources, meeting frequency, and technical support. For example, International SEMATECH is a well-known effort to roadmap progress in the global semiconductor industry. Currently it involves over 800 people participating in about 15 technical working groups over a period of a year. These participants are drawn primarily from corporations, which donate a substantial portion of the time of their employees and support the cost of the participants from their organizations because they understand that the benefits of roadmapping make this cost worthwhile both to their companies and to the industry as a whole. Also critical to the success of this industry roadmapping process is a central coordinating organization. The consortium, International SEMATECH, devotes a full-time department to focus on supporting the roadmapping process and information. Also, consortium members are prime participants in the roadmapping activities and provide additional top-down leadership by a close relationship with their advisory groups and with the member companies' implementation of the industry roadmap.

As a result of the much more limited time and resources available for the committee's work, our roadmapping effort was designed to be far less comprehensive than industry efforts, such as that of the Semiconductor Industry Association. At best, the committee could have carried out the work corresponding to that of a single technical working group of the semiconductor industry effort. However, such a focused effort would have been possible only if a previous effort in this domain had already identified what would constitute a set of discrete technical working groups. Because this had not been done in advance, the committee's work on roadmapping naturally gravitated toward the task of identifying the various components of the overall problem. In formal roadmapping terms, the committee's effort resembled the preroadmapping task, in which the domain of the future technical working groups is defined.

After its preliminary roadmapping effort, the committee's final task was to organize a workshop engaging a broad array of stakeholders and emphasizing future activities in the area of improving learning with information technology. It was necessary to find a way to communicate the many issues that had been discussed in the roadmapping effort in ways that could be discussed at a high level while being accessible in a public forum with a diverse audience. Thus, the aim of this workshop was to stimulate discussion about what future community building and strategic planning activities would be worthwhile, rather than to refine the particular items on the committee's preliminary set of roadmap tables. To facilitate this workshop discussion, the issues addressed in the committee's roadmap tables were reformulated into two "transformations":

- The first transformation deals with the infrastructure required to integrate IT into education in ways that would benefit all students. This infrastructure includes hardware and its support, professional development for teachers, access to software that fundamentally changes the ways educators think about and develop curricula, and mechanisms for providing student and parental access at home. The committee considered these issues in its roadmapping discussions, and they are presented in the Annex at the end of this chapter in Annex Tables 2-1 to 2-5.

- The second transformation deals with the research and development effort that will be required to apply findings from the scientific literature about how people learn to the next generation of educational and learning technology. These issues are considered in the committee's roadmap in Annex Tables 2-6 and 2-7.

Chapter 3 describes the January 2003 workshop discussion of these two transformations and possible next steps for establishing the technical and social infrastructures that would be needed to meld IT into K-12 teaching and learning.

Community Building

The committee's membership was initially constituted with participants from each of the three broad groups thought to be at the core of pointing the way to improving learning with information technology: K-12 educators, information technologists, and learning researchers. While each group had an interest in the goal of improving learning through information technology, they came to it with different experience, perspectives, vocabularies, and professional cultures. As a consequence, the first community building exercise took place within the committee itself. For example, during its meeting in July 2001, committee member Amy Jo Kim, who is an expert on building on-line communities (Kim, 2000), led the group in a general discussion about creating an online community to support and enhance the committee's work. She defined a web community as a group of people who have a shared purpose, interest, or activity and who get to know each other better over time. During her presentation she outlined five myths, nine "timeless" design strategies, and three design principles for web-based communities (Box 2-1).

The committee's experiences in and problems with community building turned out to be a microcosm of what is likely to happen when attempts are made to bring these three separate and well-established communities together. The committee's experiences suggest that the following questions will have to be addressed for similar efforts to be successful in the future:

- What kinds of organizational arrangements or incentives could foster ongoing collaborations among K-12 educators, information technologists, and learning scientists in ways that enable the three domains to influence each other?
- How could these three disparate communities interact on a large-enough scale to have the kind of impact needed to significantly improve student learning?

The committee's experiences and challenges with community building contributed to the design of the January 2003 workshop, the selection of invitees, and the emphasis on possible strategies and collaborations to bring about the two transformations. The design of the workshop began to facilitate among workshop participants the kind of community building that the committee had attempted to do among its own membership. For example, as detailed in Chapter 3 and Appendix B, during breakout sessions, members of all three communities worked together to establish and prioritize goals based on the ideas presented during the plenary sessions, as well as their own individual and collective expertise.

BOX 2-1 Myths, Design Strategies, and Design Principles for Developing Online Communities

Five Myths of Virtual Communities

1. There is a fundamental difference between on-line and virtual communities. (The main difference is that virtual communities are less dependent than traditional communities on their members being at a particular place at a particular time.)
2. Cutting-edge technology is always best. (Sometimes cutting-edge technology can get in the way of the community working as planned, especially if it is not readily available to all community members.)
3. Communities are based on conversations. (Conversations are often what happen in communities, but they do not form the core of a community.)
4. Communities are supportive and egalitarian.
5. Community culture can be separate from that of the organization that hosts the community.

Nine Timeless Design Strategies

1. Define and clearly articulate the purpose of the community.
2. Build flexible, extensible gathering places.
3. Create meaningful and evolving member profiles.
4. Design to accommodate a range of roles (newcomer, leader, elder, etc.).
5. Develop a strong leadership program.
6. Encourage appropriate etiquette.
7. Promote cyclic events.
8. Integrate the rituals of community life.
9. Facilitate member-run subgroups.

Three Design Principles

1. Start small and focused; grow and evolve in response to pressures and opportunities.
2. Create feedback loops between members and management.
3. Empower members over time.

ANALYTICAL CHALLENGES

The substance of the problem of improving learning with information technology also raised a number of challenges that are related to the goals described in the roadmap tables themselves. The committee discussed these challenges in the process of its preliminary roadmapping effort, which led to the current structure of the roadmap tables. An overview of these central challenges provides a useful introduction to the roadmap tables.

K-12 Decentralization

Decision making for schools is fragmented among a number of authorities: federal, state, district, and individual school. Although the most talented teachers can bring about improved learning in their own classrooms even in the absence of adequate support from authorities, the improvement in learning for all students cannot depend on the most talented teachers alone. Recent attempts to enact systemic reform, by policy makers and civic, education, and business leaders, have tried to recruit all levels of authority toward the goal of improving student learning. However, while a number of promising projects exist in schools and districts across the country, the problem of scaling them to involve large numbers of students remains an enduring problem. What strategies can be used to increase the chances that the desired improvement will happen—that it will be adopted and sustained by a critical mass of school districts over time? The disappointing news is that the systemic reform movement in K-12 education has grappled with this scaling issue for almost two decades without major breakthroughs (Fuhrman, 1994; Knapp, 1997; Shields et al., 1997). However, the good news is that the movement may provide some natural allies for the effort and insights on effective strategies for influencing the K-12 education system to exploit information technologies to improve learning and teaching (e.g., Blumenfeld et al., 2000; Confrey et al., 2000; Harvard Graduate School of Education, in press). It is possible that the uses of networked learning technologies and teacher supports, coupled with careful attention to design factors found to be affiliated with success in systemic reforms, could help contribute to more rapid uptake of research-grounded innovations.

Evidence of Success

It will be easier to secure adequate levels of political support, funding, and community buy-in for any efforts aimed at improving learning with IT if there are clear demonstrations of IT tools for teaching and learning that bring dramatic improvements in student learning. This is particularly the case if the improvements are shown using measures of student learning that matter to the stakeholders who are being held increasingly accountable for improving learning, including parents, teachers, and school administrators. This challenge has become acute in the current policy environment brought by the No Child Left Behind Act of 2001, which calls for scientifically based education research.[1]

Markets

Development and large-scale adoption of IT-enabled tools for K-12 learning and teaching are hampered by the current structure and incentives of the marketplace for education technology. One feature of this marketplace is the absence of a sufficient level of organized demand. The lack of a critical mass of demand, to which IT developers could respond, can be attributed at least in significant degree to the decentralized and uncoordinated nature of much K-12 decision making in the United States. Although most states now have student learning goals, or standards for what students should know and be able to do, or both, these differ across states. Most states also have requirements for assessment, but these too vary and frequently are independent of policies and practices related to curriculum and instruction. In addition, decisions on curriculum and instruction are overwhelmingly the province of local education authorities at the district or school levels. Finally, purchasing decisions for hardware and software tend to be fragmented among many actors, many of whom purchase relatively small quantities. A further irony is that the primary users of IT in education—teachers and learners—are typically not the buyers of IT and have little influence on buying decisions. Expecting some level of deliberate, coordinated development of IT-enabled tools tailored for K-12 use in this market environment is unrealistic. Instead, IT developers will continue to be driven by more coherent and predictable sources of demand outside education. Thus, without changes in the market conditions described above, business- and office-related applications and products for home entertainment (which sometimes include a learning component) will

---

[1]Means and Penuel (in press) note that technology-based educational innovations are often "highly dependent on implementation processes and contextual factors" that are "often neglected by studies focused on main effects." They argue that this dependence must be taken into account in the evaluations of these systems.

continue to dominate design, development, and marketing efforts, and these applications will probably continue to be used by the education community rather than tailored for it.

PRELIMINARY ROADMAPPING GOAL TABLES

The preliminary roadmapping tables in the Annex to this chapter are based on discussions at the committee's June 2002 meeting. Such efforts typically start with an examination of the current state of the issue to be roadmapped, the development of a vision of where the roadmap should lead, and goals and time lines that are needed to achieve the vision. Middle school science teaching and learning today and in the future served as the initial focus of the committee's assessments, although the conversation ranged more freely over science education in general and to the more generic contextual issues that pose problems for progress in learning across the curriculum. Many of the roadmapping goals were determined to be best stated without specific reference to middle school science, although they have applicability there as elsewhere in K-12 learning and teaching.

The committee's discussions of the opportunities for and challenges to bridging the gap between current realities and the goals articulated during the roadmapping exercise provided the detail in the form of progress points, or benchmarks, to be added to the table for each goal. These benchmarks are organized into columns for the near, mid and long term. While all items are critical and need the research communities of education and IT industry, longer term items listed serve to address the out-years and the time needed to incubate concepts and future support systems, develop policy, and spawn needed research.

In some roadmaps, the benchmarks are color-coded according to the character of the barriers identified, indicating whether the barriers are technical or nontechnical, whether they might be addressed through short- or long-term research, or whether known research solutions do not exist presently. However, many of the benchmarks on the ILIT preliminary tables are affected by a mix of barriers because they are more general than the benchmarks on other roadmaps. As a result, the committee decided that it would be clearer to discuss the nature of the barriers in the sections on challenges that precede each of the tables.

Finally, along with each table the committee included a statement of the needs that led it to formulate the goal, the challenges to and opportunities for addressing those needs, and which stakeholders might have primary responsibility for action related to the need.

ANNEX TO CHAPTER

Roadmapping Table 1: Standards-Aligned System of Curriculum, Instruction, and Assessment

Need addressed: Large-scale improvement of learning is dependent on greater customization of instructional materials and methods for individual students within a system of curriculum, instruction, and assessment aligned to standards on what students should know and be able to do.

Challenges:
- Each state determines its own learning requirements and local districts and school boards often feel proprietary about their curriculum and assessment policy. Any efforts at alignment of curriculum, instruction, and assessment are likely to require state policy leadership.
- Although schools and classrooms now are almost universally wired and equipped with computers to greater or lesser degrees, the ratio of computers to students and even for some teachers is still far from the 1:1 found in many government, nonprofit organization, and business settings.
- The cost/quantity and reliability of the technology pose significant problems for classroom teachers.

Opportunities:
- Emerging IT capabilities will allow teachers to customize curriculum, instruction, and assessment for individual students and will provide real-time feedback to students and teachers on actual student learning of content and problem-solving skills, thereby guiding teacher interventions.
- Alignment of curriculum, instruction, and assessment could help aggregate demand for such IT-enabled teaching and learning tools.
- Alignment of curriculum, instruction and assessment needs to be dynamic, that is, able to incorporate new knowledge or understanding about subject content and how people learn. IT has the potential to allow revisions of curriculum content, instructional strategies, and assessment on a continuous improvement basis.
- There are some encouraging instances of districts and schools working toward solving the problems of computer cost and reliability.
- There is a large and growing body of knowledge on how people learn that could be used to improve curriculum, instruction, and assessment and related IT tools for teaching and learning.

ANNEX TABLE 2-1 Standards-Aligned System of Curriculum, Instruction, and Assessment

Primary change agents: State and district education policy makers, federal law

Goals	Near Term (1-5 years)	Mid Term (6-10 years)	Long Term (11-20 years)
Create a dynamically aligned system of curriculum, instruction, and assessment, based on evolving learning requirements (what students should know and be able to do) and consistent with what is known about how students learn and with the capability of IT to enhance that learning.	Significant number of states and districts adopt IT-enabled curricula and related instructional strategies that are consistent with the *National Science Education Standards* (NSES); states align state science standards with NSES.	Significant number of states and districts adopt IT-enabled curricula that integrate general research on how people learn with real-world and virtual experiences and permits customization for students.	Variety of learning tools are used to customize curriculum and instruction (limited role of textbooks).
	States and districts establish quantifiable assessment objectives that are tied to curriculum and instruction.	Widespread state and district use of IT-enabled tools for both summative and formative assessments. Increasing district/classroom reliance on ongoing embedded assessment methodologies.	Ongoing embedded formative assessment reduces/eliminates need for a separate summative assessment (e.g., final exams). All students have wireless, networked computing devices to allow customized curriculum, instruction, and assessment.

Roadmapping Table 2: Teacher Education for Improving Learning with IT

Need addressed: To maximize the effectiveness of information technology in education, both new and veteran teachers must be able to make good use of technology tools for curriculum, instruction, and assessment.

Challenges:
• Many current teachers have little idea how to use technology tools to enhance teaching and learning. While they use available technologies

to increase their own personal productivity, which is a large part of a teacher's workday, they tend to continue business as usual when it comes to integrating technology into instruction.

- Colleges and universities provide new teachers with little initial preparation,[2] while meaningful teacher professional development on IT (i.e., professional development that focuses on appropriate uses of IT to enhance learning rather than emphasizing how to operate the hardware and software itself) has been a low priority for most school districts.
- The widespread nonalignment of curriculum, instruction, and assessment and the prevalence of local decision making on technology contribute to the fragmentation of demand for IT-enabled teaching and learning tools.

Opportunities:
- A broadly based consortium of organizations representing major professional education groups, government entities, foundations, and corporations has developed standards for what children, teachers, technology leaders, and other educational professionals should know about and be able do with information technology (e.g., National Educational Technology Standards [NETS] for students as well as teachers from the International Society for Technology in Education [ISTE], http://cnets.iste.org/).
- Three developments could stimulate both the supply of and demand for training in IT use for educators: (1) significantly increased numbers of cheap, reliable computers, approaching a 1:1 ratio with students in classrooms and computers on the desks of every teacher; (2) agreement on alignment of curriculum, instruction, and assessment by a significant number of states/districts so that hardware and software developers can sell to a much less fragmented marketplace; and (3) driving state accrediting bodies and/or schools of education and providers of teacher professional development to include standards for teacher IT skills as requirements.
- Web-based technologies exist that could make it easier for the teachers to take part in ongoing professional development opportunities.

Roadmapping Table 3: Networked Communities of Teachers

Need addressed: Even in the largest schools, teachers tend to be isolated in their classrooms or do not have a sufficient number of col-

---

[2] Some progress has been made with the U.S. Department of Education's program to support efforts to integrate technology in pre-service teaching and learning programs. See the website for Preparing Tomorrow's Teachers to Use Technology at http://www.pt3.org.

ANNEX TABLE 2-2 Teacher Education for Improving Learning with IT

Primary change agents: Schools of education, national and state-level accrediting organizations

Goals	Near Term (1-5 years)	Mid Term (6-10 years)	Long Term (11-20 years)
Career-long teacher education based on evolving technology standards, how people learn, and an aligned system of curriculum, instruction, and assessment.	The Council of Chief State School Officers, the Education Commission of the States, and state actions promote visibility, adoption, and implementation of existing and evolving standards for teacher IT skills (30 of 50 states and the District of Columbia have already adopted, adapted, or aligned with ISTE/NETS standards in their state technology plans, certification, licensure, assessment plans, or other state documents: http://cnets.iste.org/getdocs.html).	State teacher certification requires that all teacher candidates receive practice teaching with information technology consistent with research on how people learn.	
	Teacher education programs responsible for majority of teacher candidates require candidates to learn to use technology in the classroom in ways that are supported by research on how people learn.	Learning from on-line teacher communities (see Annex Table 2-3) is aggregated to provide feedback to teacher training institutions on needed improvements.	Information technologies are fully integrated into the university—including science disciplinary departments and in practicum learning experiences—in ways that are consistent with research on how people learn, such as integrating research with education (e.g., student-scientist partnerships).
	Design of teacher professional development incorporates combination of standards for IT and research on how people learn.	Ongoing professional development that meets the standards is routinely available in 50 percent of school districts.	Ongoing professional development that meets the standards is used by nearly all teachers in 100 percent of school districts.

PRELIMINARY COMMUNITY BUILDING AND ROADMAPPING EFFORTS 27

Goals	Near Term (1-5 years)	Mid Term (6-10 years)	Long Term (11-20 years)
	Teachers learn to use IT tools for purposes of diagnosing student learning results and of customizing curriculum, instruction, and assessment.	Teachers learn to use IT tools for purposes of gauging student motivation and for customizing curriculum, instruction, and assessment.	Data-driven recognition of patterns of student learning and motivation is used to recommend changes of curriculum and instruction.
		Investigating just-in-time and real-time web-based coaching for teachers in their classrooms from district or remote mentors observing teaching.	Best practice models of web-based coaching for teachers in their classrooms from district or remote mentors in widespread use.

leagues with similar expertise to form learning communities. For the most part, teachers do not have effective ways to share information about instructional practices, including records of practice (as in videotapes of their teaching), or in their use of IT-enabled teaching and learning tools.

Challenges: The educational system currently provides few incentives for teachers to improve their teaching practices, and schools of education and school districts rarely offer coherent programs for ongoing teacher professional development for their graduates or employees. Environments of trust and security need to be established for teachers to feel safe in sharing their work and inviting suggestions for improvements.

Opportunities: There are bodies of knowledge on teacher learning in communities, on using web-based technologies for establishing on-line communities of practice for teacher professional development, and on uses of case studies for teacher learning that could be much more broadly utilized (e.g., Barab and Duffy, 2000; Blanton et al., 1998; Cochran-Smith and Lytle, 1999; Goldman, 2001; Perry and Talley, 2001; Schlager et al., 2002; Shulman, 1992).

Roadmapping Table 4: K-12 Educational IT Product Evaluation

Need addressed: Many K-12 purchasers of technology products for schools and districts are not classroom teachers and often have little knowledge

ANNEX TABLE 2-3 Networked Communities of Teachers for Career-Long Learning

Primary change agents: Schools of education, state education departments, teacher organizations, such as the National Science Teachers Association and the National Council of Teachers of Mathematics

Goals	Near Term (1-5 years)	Mid Term (6-10 years)	Long Term (11-20 years)
Create and support networked improvement communities for career-long continuous learning for K-12 educators.	Education school faculty, state departments of education, district school leaders, and teacher organizations devise strategies for on-line teacher communities to facilitate peer-to-peer networking.	Opportunities for face-to-face teacher communities on the basis of specialized interests identified in on-line communities.	
	Teachers post text and web-log ("blog") best practices of IT use in their classrooms for peers and experiment with sharing of digital videos of their teaching online.	Broad digital libraries are available of video case studies of teaching with research-informed uses of IT.	Teachers frequently post on-line web videos of their own science teaching as part of professional video portfolio for feedback purposes with peers and mentors.
	University consortia establish support systems for all graduated new science teachers from consortia schools in communities where they teach independent of where they studied.	University consortia establish virtual networks for connecting graduates.	Career-long deep relationships are maintained by teacher training institutions and teachers through continuing education, mentoring, faculty exchanges, science internships, etc.

about product effectiveness or usability in classroom settings. Putting more product evaluation information and teacher input into the decision-making process is one way to encourage the development and adoption of products that advance learning.

Challenges: It is not clear that the current decision makers would willingly relinquish their purchasing authority. Most teachers are not experts in cognitive science or in the potential uses of IT to transform learning, so they might not know how to fully evaluate the educational effectiveness of the products they wish to purchase. In addition, the research base in education using IT has not been synthesized in a manner to readily guide school purchasing decisions of existing products or product features.

Opportunities: There are successful product evaluation services beyond the K-12 realm that might serve as useful models for the service envisioned below (e.g., J.D. Powers studies customer satisfaction for a broad range of products; Consumer Reports does expert testing of product categories and exemplars; Zagat's Guide assesses customer satisfaction with restaurants and the Michelin Guide has experts do the same; Epinions is a customer-data driven comparison shopping web site; eBay buyers rate sellers). If the service were properly structured, companies might be willing to fund it, although an argument for federal funding can also be made.

ANNEX TABLE 2-4   K-12 Educational IT Product Evaluation

Primary change agents: Teacher organizations, digital libraries

Goals	Near Term (1-5 years)	Mid Term (6-10 years)	Long Term (11-20 years)
Establish web-based forum for independent reviews of IT-enabled educational products by classroom teachers, technology purchasers, and learning scientists.	Common templates developed to provide detailed feedback on IT products, context for use, suggestions, etc. Infomediaries (Hagel and Armstrong, 1997) created for product reviews with incentives for teachers (cash, recognition).	Many categories of IT-enabled educational products are reviewed for how well they integrate research on how people learn and how well they work in the classroom.	All major categories of IT-enabled educational products are reviewed for how well they integrate research on how people learn and how well they work in the classroom.

Roadmapping Table 5: Connections to Remote Scientific Resources

Need addressed: A goal of K-12 science education is for students to understand how science builds knowledge from inquiry. One way to achieve that goal is for students and teachers to complement actual lab experiments and classroom explorations by using IT tools to access the vast and rapidly expanding body of scientific knowledge, instrumentation, experimentation, and other scientific resources that scientists use.

Challenges: Some scientific instruments are too expensive or fragile to be used in the average K-12 classroom, and some experiments are too dangerous to be performed by children. There also are currently not enough instruments and research opportunities available on the Internet to make access to them universal, and few web sites are compliant with federal requirements for universal access.[3] Many teachers are not familiar enough

---

[3]Section 508 of the Rehabilitation Act requires that federal agencies' electronic and information technology be accessible to people with disabilities, see http://www.section508.gov.

with the variety of educational opportunities and resources available remotely or with how best to integrate them into the curriculum.

Opportunities: There are many "collaboratory" projects that allow students to control expensive, uncommon, or delicate scientific instruments

ANNEX TABLE 2-5 Connections to Remote Science Resources

Primary change agents: Outreach activities for federally funded science research and museums, digital libraries

Goals	Near Term (1-5 years)	Mid Term (6-10 years)	Long Term (11-20 years)
Develop a learning grid* to provide K-12 schools with access to remote scientific resources via IT and a system to ensure sufficient remote resources are made available for all interested users.	Demonstrate the use of IT to access remote scientific instrumentation, databases, and sensor networks to permit virtual use of real physical instruments. Virtual and/or real field experiences are embedded in curriculum and instruction for all science students and meet Section 508 universal access compliance. Virtual and/or real use of science museum resources is embedded in curriculum and instruction.	Significant adoption of IT to access scientific resources. Computing grid for K-12 science implemented.	Use of IT to access scientific resources becomes mainstream. Extended computing grid implemented.

*A learning grid provides connections to on-line learning resources. In current realizations for K-12 education, the grid functions only as an index. See, for example, the United Kingdom's National Grid for Learning (http://www.ngfl.gov.uk) and the Math Forum's web site (http://mathforum.org). In the next phase of computer networking, a computing grid will harness unused processing cycles of computers in a network for solving problems that are too intensive for any single computer alone (Foster et al., 2001). Current examples of a computing grid are the SETI project at Berkeley (http://setiathome.ssl.berkeley.edu) and the protein folding project at Stanford (http://folding.stanford.ed/). The National Science Foundation's national middleware initiative (http://www.nsf-middleware.org/) and the United Kingdom's e-science grid (http://www.escience-grid.org.uk) are intended to bring the computing grid to universities and eventually to K-12 education. This future learning grid will allow students to do much more advanced work in computing-intensive applications, such as simulation and modeling.

or to otherwise engage in scientific research through the Internet. Close evaluation of these projects could yield useful information about their educational impact and how they could be replicated and scaled up. Increasingly, institutions from federal laboratories to museums are putting their materials and collections on line in ways that allow the virtual visitors to interact with the artifacts and information.

Roadmapping Table 6: Development of IT-Enabled Products for Curriculum, Instruction, and Assessment

Need addressed: Although IT products designed for entertainment and business uses are powerful and versatile enough that adaptations could be developed for applications in K-12 education, there are few market incentives for such development. There also are few incentives for the makers of these products to design new product lines on their platforms that are tailored to the needs of the K-12 education system.

Challenges:
- Home/business technologies are not optimally designed for use in education, and little is known about how to make good educational use of the products that exist or are likely to be developed for home or business use.
- Knowledge about how best to use IT for education must somehow draw on insights from research into learning and incorporate that knowledge into the design and use of new products.
- IT and the learning sciences are each advancing over time at different rates, and it is difficult to establish an alignment of learning research and product development that is subject to reciprocal influences.
- Currently, there is little incentive for learning science researchers or K-12 teachers to actively participate in the production of new IT-based curriculum, instruction, and assessment tools.

Opportunities:
- Students typically and increasingly have technologies available at home that have the potential to be used as educational devices, and those technologies tend to be more robust and user-friendly than the ones available to students at school. Students would benefit if the technologies with which they are familiar in their home/work lives also could be adapted and used as educational tools (e.g., Hoppe et al., 2002; Roschelle and Pea, 2002).
- Alignment of curriculum, instruction, and assessment in a significant number of states and districts has the potential, by generating sufficient demand, to stimulate the development, use, and continued improvement of aligned IT-enabled teaching and learning tools.

- Both information technology and learning sciences research have advanced to the point at which they could make useful practical contributions to improving teaching and learning.

ANNEX TABLE 2-6 Development and Creative Use of IT-Enabled Curriculum, Instruction, and Assessment Materials

Primary change agents: Public- and private-sector curriculum developers, subject matter learning researchers

Goals	Near Term (1-5 years)	Mid Term (6-10 years)	Long Term (11-20 years)
Create continuously improved curriculum, instruction, and assessment materials rich in creative use of IT tools that improve learning and are aligned with evolving standards of what students need to know and be able to do.	Develop IT-enabled curriculum materials for K-12 science and math disciplines that use embedded assessment to personalize instruction.	Develop cognitive models of expertise for K-12 English and social studies (understudied today). Develop additional IT-enabled curriculum materials for K-12 English, math, science, and social studies, using embedded assessment to personalize instruction.	
	Provide opportunities for teachers and researchers to participate in IT industry internships to work on products designed for K-12 market. National Science Foundation grants require or provide incentives for partnerships of researchers, IT designers, and educators for K-12 IT product development and evaluation.	Developers apply teacher best practices from networked communities (see Annex Table 2-3).	Continual communications among learning scientists, IT designers, and K-12 educators, to: -reduce the distance between research results and IT product design; and -increase mutual influence among the sectors.
	Experimental developments of curriculum and instruction modules to exploit Internet-2.	Widespread developments of curriculum, instruction, and assessment materials that use Internet-2 for learning science, such as tele-immersive software.	

Goals	Near Term (1-5 years)	Mid Term (6-10 years)	Long Term (11-20 years)
	Developers adopt dual-use design strategies to increase compatibility of IT products intended for home/business use with those for use in K-12 education in order to extend learning across space and time.	Apply standards for learnable interfaces.	
	Provide rewards and recognition systems for creating new curriculum, instruction, and assessment materials across sectors.		
		Apply tools for modifying instruction to reflect student motivation and interest (see Annex Table 2-7).	

Roadmapping Table 7: Research for the Next Generation of IT Tools to Improve Learning

Need addressed (1): Student motivation and engagement (or lack thereof) are major factors in determining how much a student will accomplish in school. Increasing students' engagement and motivation through instructional interventions, such as the use of virtual reality and other multisensory input, can lead to increased academic time on task, school attendance, and the likelihood of academic success.

Challenges: We do not have accurate technical means to measure students' levels of motivation on a real-time basis. There also are privacy issues that would be raised by attempts to record a student's motivation level.

Opportunities: Technology exists that could in principle be used to monitor, record, and analyze physical indicators that can correlate with a person's level of alertness or motivation, such as physiological indicators of arousal, eye gaze (e.g., Salvucci and Anderson, 2000), facial expression, and posture. These indicators have been used extensively in media studies (e.g., Reeves and Nass, 1996) but have not been exploited in the context of learning subject matter using information technologies.

Need addressed (2): There is no standard user interface for educational IT products. The lack of standardization increases the amount of time users (both teachers and students) need to spend learning how to use the interface and reduces the interoperability of hardware and software.

Challenges: There is a trade-off between standardization in interface design and the creativity that can be applied by individual software designers; it is difficult to know whether the right balance has been achieved. Nonetheless, federal requirements for universal access will become a driver toward such objectives and in principle.

Opportunities: IT companies have conducted a considerable amount of research on effective user interfaces, and the Digital National Library will help create standard user interfaces for the resources it will contain (see http://www.dli2.nsf.gov/).

ANNEX TABLE 2-7 Research for the Next Generation of IT Tools to Improve Learning

Primary change agents: Public/private sector learning technology researchers

Goals	Near Term (1-5 years)	Mid Term (6-10 years)	Long Term (11-20 years)
Develop capability to measure student interest and motivation in order to personalize curriculum, instruction, and assessment so learning time is more productive.	Develop models of individual and group interest and motivation in various learning situations. Develop tools to measure student motivation/interest and modify instruction accordingly.	Develop IT tools sensitive to cultural, gender, and other factors. Develop IT tools that can sense a wide range of ways of knowing and showing knowledge.	
Create coherent and learnable interfaces and resource directories for IT science learning applications to enable cross-supplier product use and minimize time to learn how to use IT tools.	Effective research-based best practice interface design standards for industry/suppliers are developed. On-line training incorporated with IT tools. Digital National Library develops platform standards for IT products.	New search engines for learning applications that use intuitive natural language interfaces.	

3

January 2003 Workshop

FIRST TRANSFORMATION

The first session of the workshop focused on the discussion of the first transformation: the challenge of integrating cheap, fast, robust computers into instruction for every student in America. The session began with three presentations. Barbara Allen and Darryl LaGace described the LemonLINK project for integrating computers into instruction in the Lemon Grove School District in California. Steve Rappaport of Advanced Networks and Services discussed some of the requirements for using technology to improve student learning. Geneva Henry of Rice University discussed the Connexions Project for creating a repository of curriculum modules in science, engineering, and mathematics. These presentations were followed by comments by Cheryl Lemke of the Metiri Group and Wanda Bussey of Rufus King High School in Milwaukee.

Integrating Cheap, Fast, Robust Computers into Instruction for Every Student in Lemon Grove, CA

Barbara Allen, of Project LemonLINK,[1] opened the workshop's first presentation with the observation that although millions of dollars have

---

[1] Additional information about Project LemonLINK is available at: www.lgsd.k12.ca.us/lemonlink.

been spent trying to implement technology in classrooms across the country over the past 10 years, too much of the education community is still waiting for it to happen. She and colleague Darryl LaGace proceeded to draw on their experience in the Lemon Grove School District to identify obstacles they encountered and to share what they suggested is a promising approach to realizing the benefits of technology-rich curriculum and instruction that could be applied in other school districts.

Lemon Grove is a community eight miles east of San Diego with 4,600 students in grades K-8, 60 percent of whom are eligible for free or reduced-price lunch. Approximately six years ago the district developed a vision for creating a truly connected learning community, with access to that community from anywhere in Lemon Grove, including classrooms, libraries, homes, and community centers. From the outset the designers of this on-line learning community saw easy and seamless access as pivotal to providing the same type of technology-enabled educational experience across all classrooms and to all students.

Their initial target for access to hardware was a ratio of one conventional computer to four students. After more than a year into the plan, it became clear that the 1:4 computer-to-student ratio was not making a difference in instruction. The computers remained literally and figuratively peripheral, while the amount of time the hardware or software was unusable or required special attention reinforced concerns that this approach to instruction and learning was unreliable. Those involved with developing this learning community concluded that unless they could achieve at least a 1:2 computer-to-student ratio, the traditional model of teacher at the head of the class, lesson-driven education would remain firmly in place. Today Lemon Grove has achieved a ratio of 1:2 and, the presenters contended, a transformed system of teaching and learning. Allen and LaGace proceeded to summarize the multiple organizational, technical, and economic obstacles their community faced and the strategies they adopted to overcome them.

First, Allen identified six challenges to integrating cheap, fast, robust computers into instruction for every student: reducing the cost of ownership; preparing teachers with high-quality, ongoing professional development; providing ready access to educational software linked to standards; involving parents and providing home access, including subsidized access; involving the people and organizations in the greater community whose buy-in is critical to achieve the vision and goals of the learning community; and, perhaps most importantly, justifying the cost of the effort by demonstrating the impact of the project on gains in student learning and achievement.

Some of these challenges relate to school district organization and operations, while others are technical in nature. The critical district-level issues include the reality that effective district-wide implementation—every school, every classroom with equal access to resources—is rare. Traditional models of use and deployment that view technology as an intellectually and physically separate activity also hamper technology's potential. Costs are also key: technical support for traditional computer installations is cost-prohibitive for many school districts, as is Internet connectivity. At the same time that costs are rising, most school districts' dollars for connectivity, equipment, technical support, and professional development are shrinking. As a result, individual schools often are left to implement technology on their own rather than as an integrated district-wide effort.

Next, LaGace introduced the equally difficult technical issues. First, there is no consensus or even a shared vision for what effective use of education technology looks like. Businesses producing technology have not understood the culture of schools well enough to adequately address their needs in the products and services they offer to the education community. Instead, education is expected to tweak equipment designed for other markets and users to make it work for schools. Lack of hardware and software standardization raises costs and creates challenges for effective professional development. Most IT departments in school districts lack expertise for planning, building, and maintaining a robust, cost-effective network and are not client oriented.

Basing his comments on experiences from LemonLINK's five-year implementation history LaGace turned to the key requirements for reaching the point at which *all* teachers in a district fully integrate technology into curriculum and instruction for daily use. These include

- equipment that is simple to operate (instant ON, like an appliance);
- fast, dependable connectivity;
- operation that is both reliable and predictable (e.g., technical support is readily available);
- tools that allow teachers to locate quality electronic resources that are aligned with standards; and
- electronic delivery of lessons, instructional materials, and resources that is easy to organize.

Most important, he emphasized, is "access, access, access." However, if access is defined as a minimum 1:2 computer-to-student ratio, then he acknowledged that access is likely to be cost-prohibitive for the approach to computer use taken by most school districts. This is especially true when the total cost of ownership of hardware, peripherals, and software is taken into account. Associated with such ownership are costs for deploying, operating, and maintaining a computer network over a period of time, including connectivity, network hardware, workstations, technical support, staff development, repairs, replacement, upgrades, software purchases, and ongoing licensing fees. For LemonLINK, fiscal realities made it essential to drive down both the costs and the complexity of the technology.

LemonLINK approached the cost issues proactively through a broad array of partnerships in order to develop a cost-effective model for computer use in schools that was not already being provided by the market. The design team took the initiative to identify the kinds of capabilities they needed and to develop their technologically based learning community as a business proposition in ways that would appeal to potential partners. Obvious partners included hardware, software, and networking providers, such as Microsoft, Hewlett Packard, and Citrix. The plan also involved working with Cox Communications, the town's local cable provider, for home connectivity. Finally, higher education institutions, including the University of California, San Diego, helped to round out their partnership strategy. Until the market provides ready access to a cost-effective model for computer use, other school districts may find it worthwhile to pursue such partnerships as well.

In another innovative approach to offsetting costs, LemonLINK has contracted to provide network services to various public-sector organizations in the community. In a prescient move 10 years ago, the district erected a communications tower, which now sends video, voice, and data across its private network, not only to the schools but also to the City of Lemon Grove, local fire departments, the community center, the recreation department, the teen center, the senior center, and the nearby charter high school, which is attended by 60 percent of Lemon Grove's graduates. Thus the district's technology budget, only about 1.9 percent of its general fund,[2] is supplemented by revenues generated from providing these services. And the community benefits from a growing, integrated, and seamless network.

Centralized network design is a key factor in LemonLINK's cost structure and effectiveness. The district's technology center allows multiple district organizations to share resources as well as to process and store data that can be accessed across the network. Because everyone's programs and data reside at the center, students and staff can be anywhere—such as at a school, in different classrooms, the local community center, or

---

[2] For comparison, the second survey of district technology coordinators conducted by the Milken Family Foundation during the 1998-1999 academic year found that on average districts spent 3.6 percent of their operating budget and 5.1 percent of their capital budget on technology (Milken Family Foundation, 1999). The survey was based on responses from nearly 3,800 districts in 27 states. The study found an average computer-to-student ratio in 1998-1999 of 1:18.5 for computers capable of accessing the Internet.

at home—and still access and manipulate their information. The centralized design concept also enables the data center to serve multiple independent organizations without the need to implement or support locally installed servers or network resources. All that is needed at a school or facility is a local area network (LAN) that can connect workstations back to the data center. The center's high availability is achieved through cluster technologies and mirrored locations. A 30 terabyte storage area network (SAN) allows teachers practically unlimited space to develop and maintain on-line curricula. Each student has a one gigabyte of space to store daily work as well as maintain an ongoing portfolio of final works.

The LemonLINK plan to supply abundant access to technology necessarily moved away from just putting more and more computers in the classroom. Instead, the district began installing smaller, cheaper network appliances known as "thin clients." By purchasing thin clients at $389 each instead of $1,500 for a multimedia station, the district dramatically increased access. This innovative approach has allowed LemonLINK to install three times more equipment in schools with the same budget allocation, and it was the key factor in attaining both the 1:2 ratio and the instant-on capability that allow teachers to focus on instruction rather than technology. While the interface is the same as that for a PC, a keyboard, a mouse, and a monitor, the thin client workstation doesn't have all the complex and expensive components of a typical PC. Most thin clients don't have any moving parts and have instant-on capabilities. Their programs and data come from "slices" of memory and processor power from a terminal services farm located at the data center. Bandwidth-intensive applications, such as streaming video, can also be viewed directly from the thin clients through LAN connections using a locally based web browser and media player. To provide for full computing capabilities, each classroom is also equipped with several multimedia workstations.

LemonLINK made an early strategic decision to get away from having schools or teachers purchase specific applications, many of which were often poorly aligned with district learning standards or were difficult to operate. Instead, LemonLINK adopted a district-wide approach whereby everyone has access to the same library of software. Currently, 15 applications are supported throughout the district. This approach has proven both effective and efficient in terms of training and support. Moreover, teachers easily share how they are using technology across schools in the district and across classrooms in schools. Technical support at the classroom level is provided on site in each school one day per week. Technical support staff participate in professional development meetings so they understand the realities of employing information technology in classroom settings. However, many technical support problems can be solved remotely. Phones in each classroom allow teachers to call the support center when a technical problem arises and receive remote help immediately, without having to submit work orders.

Staff development was designed to parallel the phased installation of the technology over the past five years. During each year of the installation period, approximately 20 percent of the teachers were provided with 100 hours of initial training, including short workshops on applications, teacher-to-teacher collaborations, observation, and hands-on use of technology in classrooms. Additional professional development is provided on an ongoing basis at the building and district levels.

What have been the results in terms of student learning? About halfway through the implementation phase, LemonLINK's outside evaluator took a very close look at student performance scores from the Stanford-9 and API state assessment data (Snyder, 2000). Roughly half the schools and students had access to technology at the desired 1:2 ratio, and their teachers were trained to use the equipment and software; the other half had not yet reached these goals. The results, reported Allen, were "astounding": students who had access to the technology did better across the board than students who did not. In some cases, she reported that the differences were striking. Matched scores on every student also allowed them to observe solid year-to-year improvements for individual students, including various subgroups, again with significant advantage to those in technology-rich classrooms. When teachers saw the results, they became far more interested in learning to use those tools in their own classrooms.

Student engagement has also benefited. In response to a question about whether technology has changed structural practices in the schools, LaGace reported on an extensive series of observations that were conducted in a recent tour of over 60 district classrooms. The object of those observations was not to observe the lessons being conducted, but rather to observe the students and what they were doing. At that time about 70 percent of classrooms were participating fully in the technology, while in about 30 percent of cases, teachers were not quite convinced of the efficacy of integrating technology into their classrooms. LaGace reported that the differences observed were striking: in the technology-rich classrooms students were engaged with their work and progressing at their own rates, collaboration was taking place, and teachers were providing instruction tailored to individual students. In the classrooms in which technology was not being used, the traditional model of teaching and learning was striking by contrast: teachers at the front of the room writing on the white board, students nodding off or otherwise distracted.

Allen also added that the configuration of the classroom has had to change: computers are now on classroom desks, not at the back of the room. The technology is part of the learning process every day, always available for searching information on a topic under discussion in class.

As technology has become a working tool in the classroom, the teacher is no longer up front but working with students as a facilitator, helping them to gain knowledge in many different ways.

Lessons have changed as well. Instead of starting with lessons that are linked to subject matter in textbooks, many teachers begin with large ideas. They then use those larger concepts to bring students to desired levels of learning through designated activities that use technology and related resources to get there. Textbooks become supplements in many cases.[3]

Finally and most importantly, according to Allen and LaGace, access to the technology and learning does not end with the school day. Currently 15 percent of district families have on-line access through LemonLINK's thin clients. With newly developed web-based access (http://mylearningportal.com), LemonLINK expects the percentage of students and families with LAN and Internet access to double as home computers connect to the network. The district also provides every student who scores below the 40th percentile on state standardized tests with a thin client for home at no cost for 12 months as an academic intervention.

The LemonLINK team shared several additional insights in response to questions:

Recruitment of new teachers: Over the five-year implementation period, teachers both retired and left the district. As new teachers have been recruited, LemonLINK is seeing a different kind of candidate. An increasingly important factor of their recruitment efforts is that teacher candidates research the school district on the web and report that they are choosing to apply to Lemon Grove because of its use of technology. One indicator is that these new teachers are themselves more technologically savvy, being able to pick up on the technology and move to a functioning level quickly—in 6 months compared with the 18 months for teachers who had participated in the 100-hour professional development program. Their interview process also emphasizes candidate compatibility with the technology-rich environment.

Experimental process in developing LemonLINK: Another question concerned LemonLINK's response to experiments in the development process that did not work. Allen was clear: if something is not working, they stop doing it. LemonLINK admits to itself and to its partners when something does not work. She emphasized that doing so is not synonymous with failure. Rather, continuing to spend lots of money without any results constitutes failure. If those who are directly involved with a project

---

[3] See Kaput and Hegedus (2002) for a discussion of some ways that classroom connectivity can allow new types of learning and teaching opportunities.

can admit to themselves that that something did not really work, they can try to understand why and learning becomes possible.

Disseminating information about LemonLINK to others: LemonLINK has received numerous visitors from other school districts. The utility of those visits depends on the kinds of people the other districts send. A team that represents different perspectives and is able to look at the challenges from different angles has a much better chance of reliably communicating what they saw and translating what they learned into action in their home districts. LemonLINK tries to focus visitors on the things that have really made a difference—what their presentation at this workshop addressed. Visitors will see the data center and the technical aspects that make the network work. But they will also see that the technical office and the curriculum/staff development/instructional methodologies offices are collocated, allowing for daily conversations. The staffs function as a team, unlike the situation for technology departments in most districts that are located apart from curriculum experts and may never have an opportunity to talk with them. Visitors also observe classrooms. By the time the visitors are finished, they should have the whole picture of what LemonLINK is and the results for teaching and learning. Once visitors return home, it is not uncommon for them to call two months later with more specific questions, especially those of a "How did you do that?" nature. LemonLINK does not have a manual that visitors can take back to their individual school boards. According to LaGace, the hardest thing for visitors to grasp is that LemonLINK is a long-term investment in change. Too often, they want to accomplish this transformation in 12 months.

Curriculum and content in the LemonLINK system: A final question turned to curriculum content. LaGace reported that an increasing amount of content is web-based and the district's own teachers are creating more and more content. In partnership with some companies, LemonLINK is working on easier ways to locate instructional materials for teachers that are aligned with standards and linked to appropriate grade levels.

Planning for Two Transformations in Education and Learning Technology

In the view of Steve Rappaport of Advanced Networks and Services, the transformation involved with integrating cheap, fast, robust computers into instruction for every student in America and ensuring that technology is integrated in ways that dramatically improve K-12 teaching and learning presents not one but two challenges. The first challenge is making technology widely available in schools and ensuring that the conditions for its effective use exist, especially technical support and professional development for teachers. The second challenge is leveraging those technological resources effectively in K-12 classrooms so that they achieve the ultimate goal of improving teaching and learning. While the two are related, each has its own issues and outcomes.

The first challenge is making technology widely available and usable by students and teachers, and the principal issues concern the nature of, access to, support for, and cost of technology. Rappaport applauded LemonLINK's successful formula for meeting his first challenge: making technology sufficiently affordable to be pervasive, reliable, well supported technically, and easy enough to use to be incorporated routinely into educational practice; and educating teachers so that they feel comfortable with technology and, more importantly, understand how to use technology effectively in their classrooms.

He readily agreed that technology has the potential for changing the way we teach and learn. He cited examples including multimedia authoring tools that have been demonstrated to increase students' means of expression, virtual tours of remote sites, simulations, and on-line collaborations. The ultimate goal, however, is to improve teaching and learning; merely placing technology in schools has a limited impact on student learning. All too often, technology is grafted onto existing teaching practices, so the result is educational practice that is technologically sophisticated but still fundamentally conventional. Rappaport pointed out that using PowerPoint instead of a blackboard or overhead projector for a presentation, for example, does not represent a fundamental shift in educational practice.

Too many policy makers view the potential of technology to improve education through a lens that focuses on efficiency, believing that schools can achieve returns on the investment in technology in education that are similar to what many businesses have realized. He cautioned against confusing efficiency with effectiveness.

Technology can make the education system more efficient in some respects, such as through improving the ability to assess student performance, marshal data in decision making, or communicate with stakeholders. For example, technology can offer significantly improved means of assessment, such as diagnostic instruments on handheld devices that allow ongoing formative assessment in classes in ways and at levels that simply cannot be achieved without technology. In addition, technology makes possible the aggregation and analysis of assessment data and hence evaluations of student performance at the school, district, state, and national levels, as well as the ability to disseminate information to parents and other stakeholders.

As was also discussed by Barbara Allen and Darryl LaGace, Rappaport stated that some evidence also exists that technology can improve student achievement. Some studies, for example, have shown increases in student performance on standardized tests (e. g. , Honey et al., 1999; Mann et al., 1998). Other studies suggest that certain types of educational software can facilitate the acquisition of early literacy skills, such as reading comprehension and vocabulary development, and that other types of software can increase students' understanding of mathematical and scientific concepts.

But it is the effectiveness of schools—that is, the ability of students to learn in them—that must remain the principal concern; and it is unwarranted to assume that merely introducing technology into educational settings will produce the desired outcome of improvements in learning. Rappaport argued that the education community has failed to demonstrate clearly that technology can improve student learning. Furthermore, he contended, a compelling case has not yet been built because educators and policy makers are asking the wrong question. While the tendency is to focus on technology and ask whether its use is improving student achievement, it is educational practices and processes that determine how well students learn. He emphasized that technology is not a process but a tool through which educational practices are mediated.

He then cited ThinkQuest,[4] a program that his organization once operated, to illustrate this point. ThinkQuest, in which over 100,000 students from 125 countries have participated, is a large-scale example of project-based learning: several students form a team, intensively study a subject for several months, and then create a web site to reflect the knowledge they've acquired. Technology makes certain things possible in ThinkQuest that could not be done otherwise, and it is a powerful motivator for students to engage in their own education. But the educational practice that is at the heart of ThinkQuest is project-based learning: students researching subjects and working on projects reflecting the knowledge they've acquired, an educational practice that predates the introduction of technology. In ThinkQuest, students use technology to complete their project, but the end-product could have been a written paper, a play, or a diorama. ThinkQuest's emphasis on project-based learning is the key, not technology.

If technology is to make a contribution to improving student learning, it must be aligned with educational practices that are most likely to achieve desired learning goals. Unless educational goals are articulated first, policy makers and educators will never understand how to align technology with educational practice to realize the goal of improving student learning. For Rappaport, the key question at this juncture is whether, as a country, the United States wants to preserve educational

---

[4]Additional information about ThinkQuest is available at: http://www.thinkquest.org/.

practices in essentially their current forms and develop ways to employ technology to increase student achievement on standardized tests, or whether the nation instead wants to take this opportunity, made possible in part by technology, to transform education in ways that will achieve dramatic improvements in student learning.

To address these questions, Rappaport argued that national organizations and the federal government must provide new leadership. A wide range of national organizations concerned with the state of education in the United States has a significant role to play in educating their constituencies and shaping the debate about the role of technology in K-12 education. Only with broad discussion among all stakeholders can a national consensus be established about the proper roles for technology in K-12 education that will allow progress on the required scale. The Consortium for School Networking,[5] for example, recently formed an emerging technologies committee to educate K-12 school leaders about advances in technologies and innovative applications of them that may enhance teaching and learning as well as school administration and decision making. The committee will also address problems of implementing and owning emerging technologies in schools, including technical issues and the total cost of ownership.

Rappaport emphasized that technology will not in itself change educational practice. It is on educational practice that efforts to improve student learning must focus. That is where the principal challenge lies.

Rice University's Connexions Project

At the heart of Rice University's Connexions Project is an electronic curriculum repository for concept-driven curriculum modules.[6] The initial content has covered courses in the sciences, engineering, and mathematics. Newer content includes music and social sciences modules, with additional humanities materials currently in preparation. Most of the existing material has been developed for college-level courses, although some of the content in music has been developed for K-12, and the system would be broadly applicable to K-12 content in other subject areas. As Geneva Henry, executive director for Connexions, explained, the concentration on concepts was a creative response to one professor's frustration

---

[5]Founded nearly a decade ago to be an advocate for improving K-12 education with telecommunications and the Internet, the Consortium for School Networking represents technology decision makers at the school district, state, and national levels. For more information see http://www.cosn.org.

[6]Additional information about the Connexions Project is available at: http://cnx.rice.edu/.

that his best-performing students had mastered the content of his course in a linear fashion that followed the textbook but missed the big ideas and unifying concepts that were his focus.

To remedy this problem, the Connexions Project was designed to stimulate authors of instructional materials to develop curriculum modules that represent individual concepts, with links included to show how the concepts interrelate. The modules are then placed in the electronic repository so instructors can explore the concepts and use them directly or modify them for use in their own teaching. Students can explore related concepts, yet stay anchored in the course they are studying. By means of open source licensing, which allows users to modify modules created by others, the project is also intended to provide opportunities for collaboration among faculty, teachers, students, and authors of material across disciplines.[7] The assumption is that many concepts may have relevance beyond individual disciplines and courses and that making them available to others to use will be beneficial.

For teachers at both the high school and postsecondary levels, the repository serves as a significant instructional resource: they can build their own courses entirely around the concepts they create or modify, or they can integrate certain concept modules into existing courses. For teachers in K-12 classrooms, easy access to rich curriculum material and the ability to adapt it to fit their needs are especially important. Aligning what the student is learning with the conceptual knowledge the teacher is trying to get across is the objective. The Connexions repository is freely open to students as well as teachers. Students can engage in general exploration of various concepts or, with the help of a set of tools developed for the purpose, can work through the course that a teacher has assembled out of multiple modules. In both cases, when students find concepts they are interested in pursuing, they will find links to related concepts that allow for easy in-depth exploration, including applications of the concepts in the world beyond the classroom. An electronic roadmap has also been developed that lets them explore without losing connection with their launch points. The objective is to engage student interest in topics that may appear as unrelated or irrelevant or isolated pieces of information when they are presented one course at a time.

---

[7]To deal with copyright issues, a Creative Comments license is attached to each module by its author. This license allows information to be made publicly available and allows people to use it and change it. All that is required is that when a modification is made to a module, the modifier carries forward the attribution of the original authors. Commercial use of the material is also permitted.

Responses

The remarks of Cheryl Lemke, president of the Metiri Group, focused on five key points. First, she agreed with Steve Rappaport that the education community must define more clearly what it means by "improving student learning." Technology is not the issue, in her view; intellectual capital and 21st century skills are. The reality is that technology has changed society so dramatically that people need to develop new skills, skills on which Metiri has been working with the North Central Regional Educational Laboratory (NCREL) in Chicago to define for the last two years. The 21st century skills are shown in Box 3-1. Lemke noted that some of them have to do with technology and some do not. However, they all reflect how technology has changed society.

Lemke then discussed the misalignment between traditional measures of student learning and 21st century skills. The charts used to demonstrate increases in academic achievement on standardized tests address the traditional conception of individual achievement. They stand in marked contrast to the commentary reported from teachers and parents: the mother who said, "My kid's a self-directed learner"; the teacher who said, "We're creating our own knowledge" and talked about project-based learning and moving her students away from learning exclusively from the textbook. Was it, Lemke asked, really the computer-aided

---

BOX 3-1 21st Century Skills

1. Digital-Age Literacy
   - Basic, scientific, mathematical, and technological literacies
   - Visual and information literacies
   - Cultural literacy and global awareness

2. Inventive Thinking
   - Adaptability/ability to manage complexity
   - Curiosity, creativity, and risk taking
   - Higher order thinking and sound reasoning

3. Effective Communication
   - Teaming, collaboration, and interpersonal skills
   - Personal and social responsibility
   - Interactive communication

4. High Productivity
   - Ability to prioritize, plan, and manage for results
   - Effective use of real-world tools
   - Relevant, high-quality products

SOURCE: NCREL, http://www.ncrel.org/engauge.

instruction, or was it the project-based learning the teachers employed? Relying on only those skills assessed in standardized tests will leave U. S. students behind in this global world. These 21st century skills are important in and of themselves, and they are also an important bridge to higher academic achievement.

Lemke's second point was that the testing environment is a huge barrier across the country. One of the things teachers report is that the standardized tests in most states actually push teachers away from using technology. The enormous emphasis on student scores on these tests puts a premium on more traditional approaches to curriculum coverage, textbook-based instruction, and test-taking strategies. She contended that the community involved with these transformations has failed to build a compelling case for how technology and 21st century skills can increase student achievement. One aspect of building that case is developing the capacity to assess these 21st century skills, an issue raised by a workshop participant.

In response, Lemke briefly described a project on which the Educational Testing Service (ETS) has been working over two years that may eventually be incorporated into the National Assessment of Educational Progress (NAEP). ETS has developed a web-based, on-line assessment for eighth graders to test their scientific inquiry skills as well as their technological literacy. For the assessment, the students work through a science tutorial on hot air balloons. In the course of the tutorial they can draw objects, observe the balloon going up and down, and graph its motion. Then they are asked three questions that require explanation. As they respond on the computer, every keystroke is tracked and the results are compared with results generated by experts. Student scores are based on their prowess in scientific inquiry and technological literacy. It is of special interest that when this assessment was tested about a year ago in New Jersey, the participating students uniformly said that it was the first time they had ever been tested and learned something at the same time. She suggested that pursuing this approach to assessment could be especially important when many are worried about the instructional time that is taken away by testing.

Roy Pea, workshop cochair, cited another research effort, funded by the National Science Foundation, that confronts some of the same psychometric challenges. Often a big issue is how to develop measures of those things that are defensible in the court of public opinion and scrutiny. The Principled Assessment for Design of Inquiry is looking in detail at component skills and scientific inquiry, trying to develop the kinds of measures that will be found adequate to that task.[8]

---

[8]See http://padi.sri.com.

In her third point, Lemke agreed with the earlier speakers on the essential conditions that have to be in place for technology to work. She emphasized leadership, an innovative culture, and the support and nurturing of those innovators. She pronounced as "unconscionable" the expectation that teachers adopt technology one at a time rather than as part of a systemic change. In an environment of high-stakes assessment, teachers are held accountable for how their students are progressing. Lemke argued that only a systems approach to making these kinds of necessary changes would yield results, as LemonLINK has shown.

The closely related fourth point concerns whole systems thinking and systems change. She reemphasized Barbara Allen's conclusion that it is not sufficient for students to have the opportunity to be taught to use technology to enhance their learning or to acquire 21st century skills because they happen to be in Ms. Jones' classes and not Mr. Smith's. Fairness demands that these changes be implemented systemically.

Lemke's final point was the importance of the one-to-one ratio of students to computers. There are some limited cases in which this is being achieved: in Maine, every seventh and eighth grader has been given a laptop and has network access at home; at a Quaker high school in Pennsylvania, the ratio of students to machines is approaching 1:2. The tipping point will occur when teachers—confronted by a classroom of students with laptops or other technology tools on their desks who are able to access a huge knowledge base—conclude they must do things differently. As the developers of LemonLINK learned, pervasive technology changes the learning environment dramatically and pushes everyone associated with the project to really do some of the new things that ought to be done. Lemke brought the message home by challenging participants to imagine having to share their computers with three other professionals. "Do you think we'd ever use it for anything that is mission critical? I don't think so. And the kids are the same way."

The second commentator was Wanda Bussey, a mathematics teacher and department chairperson at Rufus King High School in Milwaukee. She recalled that Milwaukee actually started out very well in the technology world. During the 1980s visionary curriculum specialists "dragged us kicking" into the early stages of the computer revolution. A "stutter step" followed, which corresponded closely to the problems described in Darryl LaGace's presentation on technical issues and Steve Rappaport's focus on pedagogical issues. Her conclusion: technology must be simple, reliable, supported, connected, with good resources for lessons and great infrastructure.

The need to address the total costs of ownership is especially important for schools. Early in Milwaukee's efforts, a good planning process was launched, with a hard-working technology committee that made visits and researched the technology options. They still made quite a lot of mistakes, such as purchasing two sets of laptops that are languishing in corners of classrooms because not enough teachers have figured out how to use them appropriately. These laptops are on a wireless network and could be operating immediately if the teachers could figure out what to do with that capacity. The issues of professional development are critical and Bussey commented that LemonLINK's phased 20 percent per year rule is an admirable way to approach this need.

She also expressed strong agreement with Steve Rappaport that technology needs to support what is important to the education community. She cited the development of Texas Instruments 80 graphing calculators (now replaced with the TI-73) as an example. Approximately 15 years ago, the calculus community set out to change the focus of calculus education. The leaders of this movement were wise to involve not only people at collegiate levels but also high school teachers and advanced placement (AP) teachers. At about the same time, Texas Instruments was developing a user-friendly technology that did not require a network and could be held in the user's hand. The two developments coalesced and, over the past decade, calculus, teachers, and the technology have all changed in ways that support and reinforce the others. Today, for instance, the AP calculus test is much more concept-driven. Changes in the technology of the calculator have also greatly enhanced teaching and learning. In the early days, to find an intersection of two curves, users had to "zoom in" in a series of steps. It often required a half hour of classroom time to teach students how to do so. Now the zoom-in function is a command that the technology executes quickly, freeing time for learning and discussing mathematical concepts rather than technical manipulations.

Bussey argued that the critical message of the calculus example is that the teaching methods and the content of instruction have both changed in response to the graphing calculator. Students are now able to do much more work. In calculus courses in the past, there were literally only two kinds of problems that teachers could use to teach such concepts as the length of an arc because they lacked the ability to take antiderivatives. She reminded participants about a specific calculus problem using cubic curves that appeared in most treatments of the topic several decades ago. This specific problem was used because its solution involves a perfect square, resulting in problem that can be solved easily with paper and pencil. As a result, when teachers wanted to teach students this kind of problem solving in calculus, they ended up spending far more time explaining the idiosyncrasies of this particular problem than they did in discussing what was going on in the limiting process of the arc. Graphing calculators have made that dilemma disappear. As a result, students' use of technology is allowing them and their teachers to focus more on concepts and engage in a free-flowing exchange of information and ideas. Students and their learning are the great beneficiaries.

KEY ENABLERS FOR THE FIRST TRANSFORMATION

After the presentations about the first transformation, the participants broke into four groups with an assignment to develop lists of key enablers that could help bring about the first transformation. After elaborating their candidates for key enablers within each of the breakout groups, participants then moved around the conference room, reviewing the lists of all four groups and voting for their top two choices for key enablers. The complete list of key enablers transcribed from the poster board sheets of the breakout groups is included in Appendix B. This section briefly describes the top choices.

Demonstrating the Value of Technology for K-12 Education

Several versions of this key enabler received support from a number of the participants. One version focused on the importance of assembling evidence from the research literature to show that technology enhances student achievement. Another version focused on the importance of making the case to teachers that technology can add value to their own work practices, not only by directly improving the performance of their students but also by helping them prepare lessons, interact with colleagues, and manage routine student work flow. A third version of this key enabler focused on combining these arguments about research evidence and the value of using technology for teachers to build a case for policy makers and industry officials about the types of technology use that can improve K-12 education. A fundamental aspect of this key enabler is the importance of finding ways to effectively communicate arguments about the value of technology that address the needs and expectations of different stakeholders.

Taking a Systems Approach to the Integration of Technology in K-12 Education

Several of the leading candidates for key enablers focused on the importance of addressing the full range of changes required to integrate technology into K-12 education. One of the breakout group facilitators noted the importance of the LemonLINK model in the participants' thinking about the importance of a systems approach to change. Different versions of this enabler focused on different linkages that a systems approach should bring about: one stressed the linking of curriculum, pedagogy, and technical support while another mentioned the linking of people, community, and technology.

Integrating Technology into Teacher Pre-Service and In-Service Education

Several of the key enabler candidates focused on the importance of incorporating technology into the education that teachers receive, both in their university education and in professional development activities throughout their careers. One version of this key enabler emphasized the importance of technology's being embedded in instruction for all university courses that future teachers take, including both education courses and content courses in the arts and sciences.

SECOND TRANSFORMATION

The next session of the workshop focused on the second transformation: the challenge of combining advances in the science of learning with IT capabilities to dramatically improve student learning. The session included five presentations. Louis Gomez of Northwestern University spoke about some of the capabilities of IT that would allow improved student learning and the necessary research and institutional arrangements to take advantage of those capabilities. Roy Pea of Stanford University discussed the convergence of the research, industry, and teaching communities in finding ways to work together toward using IT to improve learning and the possibility of research partnerships that would involve all three communities. James Pellegrino of the University of Illinois at Chicago spoke about the potential for evidence from the learning sciences to aid in the design of powerful learning environments that take advantage of technology. Edward Lazowska of the University of Washington discussed why past predictions that technology would revolutionize education have not been realized and why the next generation of educational software has the potential to succeed although previous technologies have failed. Robert Tinker of the Concord Consortium discussed the importance of applied research and innovation in education technology and proposed a funding outline for a balanced research agenda. After these presentations, there were additional comments by Nora Sabelli of SRI International and David Vogt of the New Media Innovation Center.

Getting Ready for the Second Transformation

Louis Gomez of Northwestern University was the first speaker to discuss what is required to bring about the second transformation: the challenge of combining advances in the science of learning with IT capabilities to dramatically improve student learning. First, he presented a vision for the kinds of IT capabilities that would allow improved student learning. Second, he outlined some of the research that is required to make the second transformation a reality. And third, he discussed the type of institutional arrangements that would be necessary to bring about these changes in both research and practice.

With regard to IT capabilities that could improve learning, Gomez first talked about the need to develop a "supportive integrated information infrastructure." This sort of information infrastructure would relieve teachers of the burden of some routine tasks and therefore allow them to focus more of their time on the activities that form the core of their work. One example of the capabilities of such an information infrastructure would be an IT system that provides students with formative feedback on written materials. This feedback would make it possible for students to have more practice developing their writing skills while reducing the time teachers spend in providing feedback about simpler matters, such as grammatical errors.

Another example of the capabilities of an information infrastructure would be an IT system that provides teachers with information about the social support services that students receive in their communities and at home. These support services often make a large impact on what children are able to do in school, but information about those services can currently be quite time-consuming for teachers to locate. A third example of the capabilities of an information infrastructure is an IT system that encourages collegiality among teachers by making it easy for them to share materials and approaches with their colleagues.

Gomez also spoke about the benefits of "developmentally rational tools." These are tools that can be used for a wide range of applications, such as visualization tools and spreadsheets. Although such tools are complex and can be ambitious to learn, their breadth of possibilities for increasing the productivity of work makes the investment in learning them worthwhile. In many cases, similar tools are used in other professions as well, and this bridge between school and professional tasks reinforces the importance of both teachers and students learning to use them.

Gomez then turned his attention to the types of research required to bring about the second transformation. This research would explore how new IT tools provide new opportunities for learning. He included several related types of research in this category: (1) understanding how increasing teachers' opportunities to learn affects the learning of their students, (2) understanding how new tools can create the capacity in an entire school community for students to undertake more ambitious work, and (3) understanding how the new tools themselves can help people understand and can be designed to take advantage of the principles and activities that have been found to work in schools.

A different type of research is related to making sense of numerous anecdotal observations and reports in which researchers and teachers discover that students who are typically not very engaged in learning unexpectedly become deeply engaged when working with an IT-supported learning system. These anecdotes offer the possibility of using better IT-supported learning to close the achievement gap for students in the United States.

Finally, Gomez discussed the issue of the institutional arrangements that are required to bring about better tool development and a new kind of research. Fundamentally, he argued for a switch to demand-side research, with a close coupling of research and practice that allows research and development to be focused on and inspired by the problems of practice. As an example of such a system, he discussed the Chicago Urban Systemic Partnership (CUSP), a city-wide system of coordinated in-service teacher professional development. It sponsors courses that are provided at universities across Chicago with a common approach. Each of these courses provides a joint focus on subject matter, student learning, and pedagogical strategies and includes preparation for integrating technology into the classroom.

Leveraging Convergences to Advance Learning and Teaching

Roy Pea, professor of education at Stanford University and cochair of the Committee on Improving Learning with Information Technology, spoke about the importance of "leveraging convergences" in order to advance learning and teaching. The concept of convergence is often used to refer to processes that are merging the different information and communication technologies, including computing, telecommunications, publishing, broadcast media, consumer electronics, photography, video, and music. However, in the context of the work of the committee, Pea emphasized the importance of a second type of convergence: the technical integration that must be pursued by industry, the research and development being advanced by the learning sciences, and the wisdom of practice from K-12 educators. By bringing together these three communities, the committee hopes to be able to stimulate innovations in learning technology that are guided by learning science research with more rapid consequence for education and learning.

As additional context for the committee's work, Pea noted the conclusions about the power of technology to support learning that came out of the National Research Council report, *How People Learn* (1999b). The learning that information technology can support includes the provision of (1) real-world problems for learning; (2) connections to experts and communities of learners; (3) visualization and analysis capabilities; (4) scaffolds

Fourth Wave Internet (adapted from Sarnoff Labs)

A multidimensional explosion

Media Richness
- Tele-immersion, Mixed Reality
- 3D interactive objects
- Audio and video
- Text and Graphics

Smart Service
- Browsers
- Search Engines
- Media based searches
- Location-based services
- Personalized Web View
- Personalized Search

Ubiquitous Connectivity
- PC connected
- Several things connected
- Everything connected
- Sensor networks

Process 100s-1000s MIPs
Storage GB-TB
Connectivity Mbps-Gbps

IT Capacity

NRC-ILIT
Jan 20, 2003

Stanford University ©
Roy Pea

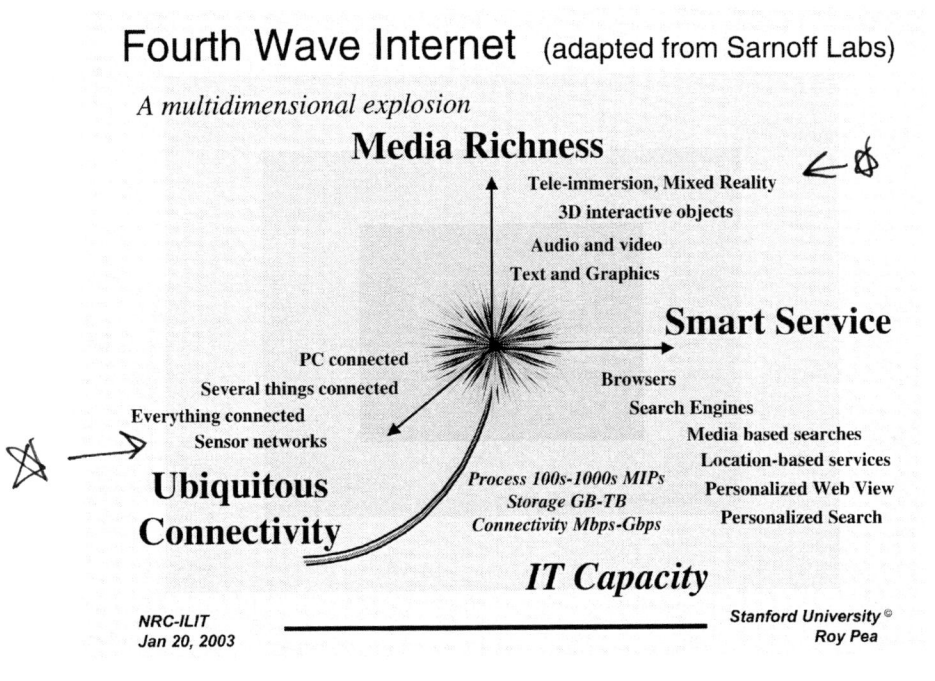

FIGURE 3-1 Changes related to IT hardware and services.

for problem solving; (5) opportunities for feedback, reflection, and revision; and (6) opportunities for teacher learning.

He then presented a diagram summarizing changes related to IT hardware and services that he originally presented at the committee's first workshop in January 2001 (see Figure 3-1).[9] These changes are driven by steady increases in IT processing power, memory, and connectivity, resulting in a multidimensional explosion in media richness and personalized software services. In the two years since presenting that diagram, there has been both continuity and evolution in the trends that it summarized. The continuity is seen in the continued exponential growth in hardware capabilities, including processor speed by a factor of 400 since 1990, memory by a factor of 120, wireless speed by a factor of 18, and fiber channel bandwidth by a factor of 10,000 (de Ruyter, 2002; National Science Foundation, 2003). One of the most interesting evolutions in these trends is the increasingly important role of the consumer market (as opposed to the business market) as a driver of commercial developments in

---

[9]Although it was not directly noted at the workshop, there is a striking contrast between the speed of technological change shown in Figure 3-1 and the "inertia" within the education system.

electronics and communications. This is seen in the explosive growth of cell phones and wireless networks. The emerging convergence of computers and telephony will soon allow tiny phone-like devices that are always connected and that are more powerful than today's PCs. These devices offer great potential for use in education, where engaging games and peer-to-peer activities can be designed to incorporate subject matter learning in compelling and adventuresome ways appropriate to the form-factor and use contexts of such devices (e.g., Hoppe et al., 2002; Roschelle and Pea, 2002; also generally see *The Journal of Personal and Ubiquitous Computing*). As a result, we see many of the big companies in this area, such as Sony, Nokia, and Microsoft, starting to look seriously at learning tools as a potentially very large and profitable marketplace. This is an opportunity that the education community needs to explore further.

Pea identified a number of capabilities that will be possible with future e-learning technologies based on these powerful and evolving trends. The declining cost of the technology will allow a one-to-one computer-student ratio with learning environments that can adapt to the learning needs and styles of individual students from tacit or explicit assessments of their needs. These personalized capabilities also will allow on-demand professional development support for teachers. In addition to allowing personalized learning environments, e-learning technologies will provide learning experiences that are rich in communication, media, and the use of complex simulation models. The technology also will allow learning that is engagement-intensive, using techniques to motivate learning by leveraging gaming strategies and the power of social networks (e.g., Barabasi, 2002). Finally, the technology will allow improved learning and teaching work flow management, including group collaborative learning tasks and embedded assessment with real-time teacher support tools and portable digital learning portfolios. These will make it possible for teachers and technologically enhanced learning environments to personalize the learning experience for students based on a rich understanding of what each student knows and is able to do.

The development of these e-learning technologies will require a broad base of research. Pea stressed that while systematic clinical trials are a worthwhile activity, they represent an end point of a complex and multifaceted research pipeline. This research pipeline includes basic research in the learning sciences, work on the construction of tools and platforms, development of proof-of-concept demonstrations for technical innovations, design research and the development of IT-based curricula and educational applications, and implementation research on the factors that influence the use and success of newly introduced techniques.

He also stressed the importance of developing new approaches to research that will bring together as partners the communities of industry and K-12 practitioners with the work of researchers in the learning sciences. The concept of finding ways to build partnerships that bridge these communities has been fundamental to the work of the committee. Such joint work will make it possible to develop more coherent approaches to the development of education technology, and it will allow the end users of that technology to make more strategic decisions about what they purchase, how they use it, and what type of professional development support they provide in conjunction with it.

One critical outcome of deeper partnerships will be in encouraging a stronger focus on "use-relevant" research, which Donald Stokes originally propounded in his book *Pasteur's Quadrant* (1999). The importance of such research was also emphasized in many of the presentations that were delivered at a workshop organized by Geneva Haertel and Barbara Means (2000) to consider the methods and approaches needed to improve research and development in the area of education technology. Such use-relevant research would involve multiple related studies conducted in networks of test-bed schools. These school sites would be committed to participating in sustained studies of the effects of technology, and they would simultaneously provide evidence of emerging trends in the use of education technology. Such large-scale research using networks of schools would require intermediary organizations to coordinate the research effort by identifying research questions, designing common data collection protocols, and supporting local researchers.

One version of such research efforts using test-bed schools has been described using the term LENS (Learning Expeditions in Networked Systems) partnerships. The term harkens back to expeditions carried out to explore the frontier during the early history of the United States, such as that by Lewis and Clark 200 years ago. The goal of LENS partnerships is to undertake expeditions to scout the future of learning. LENS partnerships would explore systemic approaches to change in education, aligning standards, curriculum, pedagogy, assessment, teacher development, school culture, and school-home connections, in addition to the use of education technology. The partnerships would undertake a continuous innovation cycle for education techniques and technology, in which the design of new prototypes would be followed by observation of the use of those prototypes, which would immediately feed back into modifications in the prototype designs.

Pea finished his remarks by returning to the concern with learning that is at the heart of any effort to improve education. At the center of the mathematics, science, and technology standards that have been developed in recent years is a concern with what some have called 21st century skills. These involve two clusters of skills: one involving seeking, organizing, and evaluating information and the other involving communicating and collaborating with others. One of the most important capabilities that new education and learning technologies make possible is the ability to provide more meaningful assessment measures for these 21st century skills, which will, in turn, allow their role in the curriculum to be increased.

Issues in Combining Advances in the Learning Sciences with IT Capabilities

James Pellegrino of the University of Illinois at Chicago began his talk by discussing the importance of building the links between research and practice. From analyses in previous studies at the National Research Council, such as *How People Learn: Bridging Research and Practice* (National Research Council, 1999b), there is only a weak relation between research on teaching and learning and actual classroom practice. Usually research affects practice only indirectly through its intermediate effect on educational materials, pre-service and in-service education, policy, and the media. Instead of the current weak and indirect relationship, Pellegrino emphasized that work is needed to create a cumulative knowledge base about classroom teaching and learning that both affects classroom practice directly and is drawn from issues, problems, and studies of classroom practice.

He then turned to discussing research on the development of expertise and competence in particular subject matter domains, such as mathematics, science, and reading. He argued that some of the most important implications for curriculum, assessment, and instruction come out of learning and cognitive research in specific curriculum domains. The fundamental lesson is that expertise is not generic but is essentially related to specific domains. One way to bring about a more coherent alignment of curriculum, assessment, and instruction is to make sure that all three are connected to understandings of how people learn in specific domains rather than to generic models of teaching and learning. However, it is important to note that the current knowledge base in learning science has developed domain-based models for only parts of the K-12 curriculum, with large portions of the curriculum having very little coverage. This underlines the importance of pursuing a vigorous research agenda to develop a full range of domain-based understandings of learning across the K-12 curriculum.

In addition to research on the development of expertise, *How People Learn* also describes what research in the learning sciences has revealed about the features of powerful learning environments. Pellegrino summarized this in four points. First, a powerful learning environment should be *knowledge centered*, with a focus on the important things we want people to learn in a given area. Second, it should be *learner centered*, so that it deals with where the learner is and can thereby respond to the needs of the learner. Third, it should be *assessment centered*, taking serious account of the processes of assessment to identify what students know and don't know so that instruction can be designed appropriately. And fourth, a powerful learning environment should be sensitive to the *social aspects of learning*, which evidence suggests are extremely important to people's acquisition of expertise.

He then described different capabilities of education technology that allow it to map onto the various aspects of powerful learning environments. Technology can enable the production of new curricular materials and instructional resources that are more focused on the key knowledge constructs that educators want students to learn. Technology also enables educators to integrate assessment into instruction, manage complex learning environments, and design modular learning and instructional resources that can be used in a variety of contexts.

He next provided more detail about opportunities to use technology to design more powerful and useful assessments that capitalize on new research about cognition and measurement. One opportunity is to use technology to provide problem-solving scenarios that tap into more complex forms of knowledge and reasoning. Another opportunity is to use technology to help interpret observations about complex student performance, such as work with E-rater®[10] and latent semantic analysis, which allow computers to score student writing (e.g., Kintsch et al. , 2000). A third opportunity is to use technology to connect assessment with instruction, with such systems as the Carnegie intelligent tutors, Diagnoser,[11] IMMEX,[12] and Summary Street[13] (e.g., Minstrell, 2000; Vendlinski and Stevens, 2002). He noted recent integrative work by Black

---

[10] E-rater® is an automated essay evaluation system using natural language processing that has been developed by Education Testing Service (Burstein, 2001).

[11] *Diagnoser* is a computer-based formative assessment tool to support instruction in physics. It is based on the idea that students come to instruction with initial ideas and preconceptions about the physical world that can vary in their appropriateness. Both before and during instruction it is useful for teachers to identify and build on these understandings. The software program helps determine what students understand and suggests ways in which instruction might then proceed. More information about *Diagnoser* can be found at: http://depts.washington.edu/huntlab/diagnoser/facet.html.

[12] *IMMEX* (Interactive Multimedia Exercises) is a set of software tools for assessing complex problem-solving strategies in areas of science. It has been used at levels that range from middle school through college and medical school. *IMMEX* consists of tools for authoring complex, multimove problem-solving tasks and for collecting performance data. The moves an individual makes during problem solving are tracked and can be represented graphically, as well as compared against patterns previously exhibited by both skilled and less skilled problem solvers. More information about *IMMEX* can be found at: http://www.immex.ucla.edu.

[13] *Summary Street* is an educational software system that uses latent semantic analysis (LSA) to support writing and revision activities with students at the middle school level and above. It provides various kinds of feedback, primarily about whether a student summary adequately covers important source content and fulfills other requirements, such as length. The feedback allows students to engage in extensive, independent practice in writing and revising without placing excessive demands on teachers for feedback. More information about *Summary Street* and other LSA-based tools can be found at: http://lsa.colorado.edu/.

and Wiliam (1998) suggesting that effective formative assessment can improve student learning by 0.4-0.75 standard deviations as determined in a variety of end-of-course achievement measures. In addition to improving student learning, such embedded formative assessment offers the possibility of reengineering current models of assessment so that information is obtained from performances proximal to the teaching and learning process. Under some scenarios in which technology supports the integration of teaching, learning, and assessment processes, it may no longer be necessary to divert attention away from ongoing teaching and learning activities so that students can prepare to be tested on external accountability or so-called drop-in-from-the-sky measures of achievement. Instead, the information needed for various assessment purposes might be derived more directly at the classroom and school levels from data streams derived from technology-based learning activities.

Finally, Pellegrino discussed some of the types of research that are necessary to make full use of technology to improve learning. He mentioned the need for research that differentiates among various technology-based tools with respect to their relative impact on teaching and learning, including attention to their respective costs and payoffs. This includes study of the impact and cost-effectiveness of general tools such as browsers, presentation programs, and spreadsheets versus tools with a content focus of a domain-general (e.g., Geometer's Sketchpad®[14]) or domain-specific (e.g., Worldwatcher[15]) nature. There is a need to better understand how much impact we can achieve with tools that do and do not draw on knowledge of domain-specific teaching and learning issues.

He also drew a distinction between research focused on designing technology-based solutions, in which the goal is to understand the impact of the software on what students can learn and understand, and research focused on understanding the conditions impacting implementation and use of those systems, such as teacher knowledge, infrastructure, and organizational constraints. He also discussed the importance of having a

---

[14]*The Geometer's Sketchpad®* is a dynamic construction and exploration tool that enables students to explore and understand mathematics in ways that are not possible with traditional tools. It is capable of being used with students from the primary grades through college. With *Sketchpad*, students can construct an object and then explore its mathematical properties by dragging the object with the mouse. More information about *The Geometer's Sketchpad®* can be found at: http://www.keypress.com/sketchpad/.

[15]*WorldWatcher* is a supportive scientific visualization environment that allows students to explore, create, and analyze complex geographic data. Its goal is to provide students in grades 6-12 and college with access to the same features found in the powerful, general-purpose visualization environments of the type that scientists use while providing students with the support they require to learn about scientific data through the use of the tools. More information about *WorldWatcher* can be found at: http://www.worldwatcher.northwestern.edu.

support structure for education research so that each new education research project isn't forced to reinvent the school-based partnerships necessary to carry out research. The requirements of such a research support structure have been described in the National Research Council's study for a Strategic Education Research Partnership (National Research Council, 1999c, 2003).

Next-Generation Educational Software

Edward Lazowska of the University of Washington began his talk by discussing the numerous examples of failed predictions that technology would revolutionize education. These include predictions about the impacts of film, radio, and television. In each case, initial hype was followed by a struggle to produce material for the new medium, then by a more mature judgment about the capabilities of the medium, and finally by a sense of disappointment and cynicism. This cycle was renewed with each appearance of a new technology.

Since computers have already passed through several stages of hype about their potential for affecting education, it is reasonable to ask why we should believe that this time will be any different. Lazowska discussed several reasons that he believes make this time particularly promising for the ability of information technology to have a substantial impact on K-12 education. First, he stressed the importance of the progress in the learning sciences over the past few decades. This work has not yet been effectively exploited by education in general or education technology in particular, leaving a huge opportunity for educational gains. Second, there is the tremendous power of the hardware advances that is typified by Moore's law, which describes the doubling of transistor density on integrated circuits every couple of years. Although that progress is continuous, we tend not to notice it until it suddenly crosses some threshold. He cited the Internet as an example of this process, going through regular doublings since its inception in 1969 but not bursting into public consciousness until it reached a critical mass in about 1993. Third, he stressed the importance of networks and the Internet in connecting people, allowing exploration, interaction, and the creation of communities in ways that previous technologies have not allowed. Fourth, he observed that the education community is moving toward a more widespread understanding that the focus of education technology should be on teaching and learning, not on the technology itself. Finally, he noted that in the current sophisticated media environment, students are accustomed to engaging media and communication technologies. This level of comfort by users with the technology itself will provide a strong demand for learning environments that are more engaging than traditional instruction.

Lazowska then turned to the kind of capabilities that are offered by information technology. First, he listed a number of capabilities that he described as "boring" because their function is straightforward. These capabilities include accessing information, publishing information, collaborating with others, building communities with others, improving class and school administration, adapting materials for learning disabled and physically disabled students, and making use of remote scientific instruments. Although the technologies involved in providing these capabilities are not particularly exotic, they can be used to provide a much more engaging learning experience for students and a broad base of support for teachers. Fundamentally, it is the provision of these "boring" capabilities that is at the heart of the first transformation, which must address huge deployment, integration, and support issues.

He then discussed the more complex and "exciting" capabilities that technology can provide. One of these is the ability to create self-paced and adaptive learning systems. These offer the possibility of simulating the kind of effective intervention and personalized instruction that individual human tutors are able to provide, which has been shown to substantially increase student learning. Such systems also offer the possibility of incorporating ongoing formative assessment that would reduce the need to devote large portions of classroom time to student testing. Finally, technology offers capabilities for complex simulations, exploratories, and clip models. Lazowska illustrated this point with several examples of web-based models providing simulations of phenomena in physics.[16] Later in his talk, he also mentioned the example of the Digital Human project, a sophisticated multilevel simulation of the human body that the Federation of American Scientists is trying to advance.[17]

The research in technology that was necessary to develop these more complex technological capabilities is substantial. Lazowska referred to these as "multidisciplinary grand challenge scale problems." In contrast, it is instructive to compare the level of research in education as a fraction of total expenditures with that in other industries. For example, the semiconductor industry's research share is over 80 times that of education.[18] In the report on education of the President's Information Technology

---

[16]See http://www.forceandmotion.com.

[17]Additional information about the Digital Human initiative is available at: http://www.fas.org/dh/index.html.

[18]The report of the President's Committee of Advisors on Science and Technology (1997, Section 8.4) noted that the United States in 1995 invested less than 0.1 percent of its spending for public K-12 education on research to determine what educational techniques work and how they can be improved. In contrast, the National Science Foundation (2002, Table A-20) reports that in 1999 the semiconductor industry invested 8.3 percent of its net sales on research and development.

Advisory Committee (2001), the overriding recommendation was to make the effective integration of information technology with education and training a national priority. That report called for the establishment of a major research initiative for information technology in education and training. Lazowska stressed that this step has not yet been taken: the technology offers tremendous opportunities for the next generation, but a serious research and development effort that could realize those opportunities has not yet been achieved.

Education Transformations Enabled by Technology

Robert Tinker of the Concord Consortium focused his presentation on applied research and innovation that meld work in technology, the learning sciences, and educational practice. He argued that these form a crucial missing link between the earlier stages of basic research in cognitive science and new technology and the later stages of dissemination and professional development. This intermediate stage includes the development of educational applications and IT-based curricula, along with research specifically focused on implementation. This intermediate stage is essential to bring about the major advances in education that technology makes possible. However, such efforts currently are both underfunded and often entirely overlooked in policy debates. He stressed that meaningful change in classrooms does not come from a single development but instead from a series of insights and innovations that cascade and evolve from more basic to more applied research.

Tinker described implementation research as being somewhat similar to medical field trials. Done correctly, it should include large numbers of students and teachers and focus on in-school studies. As an example, he described the Concord Consortium's Modeling Across the Curriculum[19] study of the use of computers to model different areas of science, which involves 13 schools and 10,000 students. The study employs a consistent approach to modeling across high school courses in biology, chemistry, and physics. It also uses random assignment of students into two different versions of the modeling approach, one more open-ended and the other more structured. The study has received $7 million in funding from the Interagency Education Research Initiative, a jointly supported project of the National Science Foundation, the U. S. Department of Education, and the National Institute of Child Health and Human Development. He stressed that this is the first time that this level of support has been supplied for this kind of serious implementation research.

---

[19]Additional information about the Modeling Across the Curriculum study can be found at the Concord Consortium's web site at: http://mac.concord.org/.

In addition to inadequate support for implementation research, Tinker also noted that innovations themselves are not being funded. He outlined the funding structure and emphases of the Math/Science Partnerships, the various national laboratories, resources and systemic initiatives, and the Centers for Teaching and Learning. Although these efforts are important, they focus on implementing, disseminating, and providing professional development for innovations that already exist, not on creating new innovations. He likened this to funding the construction and employment of a big conveyor belt without offering support for developing the goods that would be placed on the belt. Such innovation research will not come from the researchers who are engaged in basic research or from business or from the schools.

Tinker also described an idea that he called "education accelerators." These would be interdisciplinary research centers for applied, school-centered research. The accelerators would promote, support, and study large-scale, theory-based change that is supported by existing research evidence. Because such large-scale change is inherently risky, the education accelerators would provide a system of insurance and assurance, with ongoing formative assessment built in to provide an early warning system that would mitigate the risks of change and make sure that any mistakes involving students would be quickly corrected. He envisions that such research centers would receive base funding for staff and for a general research agenda with 5-year renewable grants. However, the bulk of their funding would come primarily through peer-reviewed grants to affiliated institutions.

Tinker concluded his remarks by outlining the level of funding that he believes would represent a balanced research agenda for research related to education technology. This research agenda would span the range from basic cognitive research to innovation in technology, software and curriculum, implementation research, a set of education accelerators, to human resource development at all levels. Box 3-2 reproduces his funding outline, giving an order of magnitude estimate of

---

BOX 3-2 Funding Outline for a Balanced Research Agenda in Education Technology
- Basic cognitive research: 75 projects at $200K/year = $15 million/year
- Technology innovation: 50 projects at $500K/year = $25 million/year
- Software innovation: 50 projects at $1 million/year = $50 million/year
- Curriculum innovation: 50 projects at $1 million/year = $50 million/year
- Implementation research: 50 projects at $2 million/year = $100 million/year
- Education accelerators: 10 accelerators at $5 million/year = $50 million/year
- Human resource development: 200 projects at $50K/year = $10 million/year
- Total cost: $300 million/year for 10 years

funding required for the different types of research. The outline shows that only one-third of the funding would be used to support the cognitive, technology, and software-related research that is typically thought to be the focus of education technology research. Two-thirds of the proposed funding would foster curriculum innovations and different types of implementation research that focus on the use of that technology in classrooms.

Tinker finished his presentation by noting that this level of funding is small compared with the size of the education enterprise itself, and it is about the same order of magnitude as the current efforts being spent to implement, disseminate, and provide professional development for innovations that already exist. Despite the relatively modest size of this proposed investment, he believes it has the power to transform learning in K-12 education.

Responses

Nora Sabelli of SRI International spoke as an invited commentator. She stressed the importance of conducting research on the adaptation process that is central to change in education. In this context, she noted that it is unreasonable to expect teachers to aggregate pieces of curriculum from different software developers; such aggregation must be part of the solution that the research and development community provides. She also noted that the adaptation process in schools usually doesn't involve a single innovation but rather a complex of innovations in curriculum, instructional materials, and pedagogy. As a result, it is important to think about aggregating innovations in ways that are easy for schools to adopt.

In addition, Sabelli talked about the importance of carrying out long-term research to understand the processes of educational change. She argued that typical collaborations between a researcher and a set of teachers are so short and perfunctory that they are over before the researcher and the teachers adequately understand each other's needs and potential for contributing to solutions to the problems that they should be addressing together.

David Vogt of the New Media Innovation Center also spoke as an invited commentator. In his remarks, he stressed the importance of allowing students to own their learning experiences. He contrasted this "pull" model of education with the current "push" model in which students are not in control of their own learning experiences. He argued that introducing a dynamic push-pull tension into education would make an enormous difference in students' enthusiasm and participation. As an example of work that would be relevant to a pull model, he briefly described industry entertainment research in gaming and collaboration that could be adapted to education. He argued that students already have a high level of sophistication with information technologies and that if they are not given control of their own educational experience, they will simply take that control on their own.

KEY ENABLERS FOR THE SECOND TRANSFORMATION

As was done for the first transformation, four breakout groups developed lists of key enablers after the presentations dealing with the second transformation. Participants then voted for their top two candidates. The complete list of key enablers transcribed from the poster board sheets of the breakout groups is included in Appendix B. This section briefly describes the top choices.

Defining Goals for Research and Development to Improve Learning with Technology

The discussion in one of the breakout groups identified the fundamental change required for the second transformation as the creation of an ongoing system that allows education to be continually improved through research. A leading candidate for a key enabler of this change was to define a set of targets for research and development that can motivate people, coupled with intermediate milestones to make it clear when progress has occurred. One important aspect of the definition of goals is that it be done in a way that engages the public so that there is broad public and policy support for a vision of the improvement in learning that is possible from research and development in the use of technology.

Supporting Large-Scale and Long-Term Research and Development Efforts

Several versions of this key enabler received support from a number of the participants. One version referred to targeted test beds that would focus on proof-of-concept support for the first transformation. Another version referred to the LENS partnerships discussed by Roy Pea in his presentation. A third version referred to the creation of technology parks whose mission would be to focus on the use of cognitive science and technology to improve education. These would be similar to university-industry partnerships in science, medicine, and engineering, with open sharing of intellectual property and involvement by teachers and graduate students.

Developing New Assessments

Several groups included versions of this key enabler, which recognizes the driving role played by assessment in the education system. One version mentioned the importance of conducting research and development on formative assessments, while another version mentioned moving beyond paper and pencil assessments. Some of the discussion mentioned the potential to use IT-supported tools to assess more complex 21st century skills, which would in turn allow greater emphasis to be placed on those skills in the curriculum.

Creating a Functioning Market for Education Technology

Several groups included key enablers addressing issues about the market for education technology that prevent research from being translated into goods and services. One group mentioned possible changes in the tax structure. The discussion in another group focused on creating a forum to reconcile the divergence in views between suppliers who argue that there is no coordination of requirements for purchasing and K-12 practitioners who argue that suppliers do not understand or care about their particular needs. Finding a resolution of this impasse could open a substantial market to industry while providing transformational tools to education practitioners.

NEXT STEPS FOR THE NATIONAL ACADEMIES

The final session of the workshop focused on a discussion of the ways that the National Academies could partner with teachers, industry, learning researchers, and policy groups to help bring about the two transformations in the use of information technology to improve learning. The session began with invited comments by Milton Goldberg of the Education Commission of the States, Marshall Smith of the Hewlett Foundation, Terry Rogers of Advanced Networks and Services, and Michael Feuer of the National Research Council. Following their individual comments, the discussion was opened to all workshop participants.

The following summary of six suggestions integrates the invited comments of the different speakers along with the general discussion. This format brings together related comments that were made at different times by different speakers.

Assessing Effective IT Uses and Tools

A number of the participants commented that it would be useful for the National Academies to identify effective uses of IT in K-12 education and raise awareness about promising IT tools that have been developed but are not widely known or used by schools.[20] Marshall Smith noted that there are a number of high-quality and highly effective IT tools available that educators do not know about and therefore do not use. Henry Kelly of the Federation of American Scientists noted that one of the comparative advantages of the National Academies is in being able to serve as a neutral arbiter in identifying what is new and different about these particular tools. In addition, Smith suggested that the National Academies could conduct design projects related to important areas, such as English-language learning, to describe how existing IT capabilities could be combined to meet pressing educational needs.

Milton Goldberg spoke about the importance of disseminating information from existing National Research Council reports that relate to the use of IT to improve learning. He suggested that it would be useful to form partnerships with constituent groups to explore ways to make the information in such reports more widely accessible. In addition, he underlined the importance in the current budget climate of helping state policy makers understand what technology can do to improve education.

Larry Snowhite of Houghton Mifflin Company suggested that it would be helpful for the National Academies to work jointly with policy makers and industry to facilitate the application of research findings to the development of educational materials. Several other participants argued that the National Academies could play a useful role in identifying the IT tools that are available and defining some criteria for the adoption of those tools. Roy Pea spoke about the possibility of using the convening power of the National Academies to provide a way for the publishing and research communities to work together.

Identifying Policies That Promote Effective Use of IT

In addition to identifying effective IT uses and tools, some participants noted that the National Academies can help identify policies that facilitate or hinder the use of those IT uses and tools. One aspect of helping to identify policies that promote effective use of IT would be to conduct a cost-benefit analysis of various IT approaches, along with research that demonstrates the effectiveness of employing IT to improve learning. Goldberg argued that this is an important role for the National Acad-

---

[20]It has been pointed out that there would be value in developing a theory and related frameworks that would be predictive of the uses of technology in different ways. One example of such a theory is the Evidence Centered Design model (Mislevy et al., 2003) that is being operationalized by the Education Testing Service and other investigators.

emies to play. As a negative example, Michael Feuer discussed one of the side effects of accountability testing, which is to hinder the ability of teachers to use more creative approaches in their teaching if they aren't convinced those approaches will lead to direct improvements in test scores. This comment echoed the earlier comment by Cheryl Lemke that the pressure of high-stakes tests often leads teachers to reduce creative uses of technology.

Defining a Research Agenda

Kelly noted that one of the areas of comparative advantage for the National Academies is in defining a research agenda. There were many other comments that referred to the importance of defining a research agenda while stressing the importance of focusing that agenda on issues of particular concern. Goldberg suggested a focus on the achievement gap as a way of defining a research agenda for the use of technology in education that addresses issues that people care about. Smith noted that providing accommodation in special education is the one area in which technology already has had a large impact.[21] He argued that a research agenda for the use of IT in K-12 education should be focused on similar targeted areas, such as reducing the achievement gap and using speech and language technologies to help English language learning. Steve Rappaport agreed that there had been far too little emphasis in the workshop discussion on people who have been left behind. Roy Pea discussed the inclusion provisions of the No Child Left Behind Act of 2001, arguing that they provide an opportunity for researchers, industry, and teachers to come together to find ways to use technology to improve the learning of those students who have not been making adequate progress with more traditional approaches to teaching and learning.

Terry Rogers provided a different theme for focusing a research agenda: he argued that it would be helpful to identify the hard questions that must be answered to realize the dream of using IT to transform K-12 education. As one example, he suggested the question of defining the teacher's role in an educational environment that takes full advantage of technology's ability to personalize the learning experience for students.

---

[21] In many ways, the coming together of researchers, IT developers, teachers, and parents, focused on improving learning opportunities for special education students, exemplifies the kind of community building that the committee hopes can be applied in other efforts to employ technology to advance student achievement.

Identifying Research Designs for Testing IT Applications That Are Appropriate to Different Types of Research Questions

Feuer discussed the current policy focus on scientifically based research in education and suggested that the National Academies could help construct appropriate research designs for demonstrating the effectiveness of IT applications. Goldberg elaborated on this point to note the importance of understanding when a clinical trials approach is appropriate and helping to communicate that importance to local policy makers who would be involved in such trials. Several participants argued that it is important to think carefully about appropriate research designs in relation to the speed of technological change. Pea discussed the difficulty of producing relevant results with long-term research designs when the technology being tested is changing rapidly. Smith noted the difficulties involved in a proposed clinical trial of computer tutors that would not have completed testing until the underlying technology was a decade old.

Investigating Market Failures in Education Technology

There is widespread and long-standing concern that the market for education technology is broken in some fundamental ways. Feuer noted that the former Office of Technology Assessment issued a report in 1988 that made this claim. Snowhite spoke about the frustration that publishers feel in dealing with the education market, because of the uncertainty introduced in spending decisions by political pressures. Rogers commented on the wide gulf separating the expectations of practitioners and industry representatives for education technology products. He argued that it would be helpful for the National Academies to carefully investigate this market failure and to broker a new understanding between industry and K-12 education about their respective needs. He referred to the morning's discussion of the LemonLINK project as an inspiring example because of the project's decision to negotiate with industry to obtain hardware and services that would work for them. He suggested that the National Academies could play an important role by focusing on difficulties with the market for education technology and identifying solutions that have been proposed.

Applying Research on Organizational Change to Understand Change in K-12 Education

Rogers discussed the separation of researchers and teachers in K-12 education. In particular he commented on the lack of ownership felt by K-12 practitioners in the current body of education research, which is perceived as coming from outside the community it is attempting to influence. He contrasted this separation with the organizational research literature on how innovations are developed and used and how organizations evolve and make progress. He stressed that there are important lessons to be learned from this literature, many of which are probably applicable to research in education. In particular, he argued that the literature shows that innovations are unlikely to be successful when the people who implement them are entirely separate from the researchers who design them. Although a gulf between researchers and practitioners can also arise in industry, there are usually management structures in industry that attempt to bridge the gap. No corresponding organizational structure works to bridge the gap between research and practice in education.

In general, the comments discussed during this final session of the workshop indicated that participants believe there is an important ongoing role for the National Academies to play in helping to bring about the two transformations in the use of information technology to improve learning in K-12 education. These comments share an agreement that the convening power of the National Academies can bring clarity to a number of difficult issues related to the use of IT in K-12 education. At the same time, participants were concerned that the National Academies find ways to bring together researchers, teachers, and industry representatives so that the findings from National Research Council studies can be effectively used by the entire community.

References

Barab, S.A., and Duffy, T.M. (2000). From practice fields to communities of practice. In D. Jonassen and S. Land (Eds.), *Theoretical foundations of learning environments.* Mahwah, NJ: Erlbaum.

Barabasi, A. (2002). *Linked: The new science of networks.* Cambridge, MA: Perseus.

Black, P., and Wiliam, D. (1998). Assessment and classroom learning. *Assessment in Education, 5*(1), 7-73.

Blanton, W.E., Mooreman, G., and Trathen, W. (1998). Telecommunications and teacher education: A social constructivist review. In P.D. Pearson and A. Iran-Nejad (Eds.), *Review of Research in Education, 23,* 235-275.

Blumenfeld, P., Fishman, B.J., Krajcik, J., and Marx, R. (2000). Creating usable innovations in systemic reform: Scaling up technology-embedded project-based science in urban schools. *Educational Psychologist, 35*(3).

Boesel, D. (2001). (Ed.). *Continuing professional development.* Washington, DC: National Library of Education. Available: (www.ericsp.org/pages/digests/ConProfDev.pdf).

Burstein, J. (2001). *Automated essay evaluation with natural language processing.* Presented at the conference of the National Council on Measurement in Education, April 12, Seattle, WA.

Cattagni, A., and Farris, E. (2001, May). *Internet access in U.S. public schools and classrooms: 1994-2000.* (Publication #NCES 2001071.) Washington, DC: U.S. Department of Education, National Center for Education Statistics. Available: (http://nces.ed.gov/pubsearch/pubsinfo.asp?pubid=2001071).

Cochran-Smith, M., and Lytle, S. (1999). Relationships of knowledge and practice: Teacher learning in communities. In A. Iran-Nejad and P. Pearson (Eds.), *Review of Research in Education, 24,* 251-307.

Confrey, J., Castro-Filho, J., and Wilhelm, J. (2000). Implementation research as a means to link systemic reform and applied psychology in mathematics education. *Educational Psychologist, 35*(3).

Darling-Hammond, L., and Sykes, G. (1999). (Eds.). *Teaching as the learning profession: Handbook of policy and practice.* San Francisco, CA: Jossey-Bass.

De Ruyter, B. (2002). *Challenges for end-user development in CE devices.* Eindhoven, The Netherlands: Philips NV Research Labs.

Education Week. (2000). *Quality counts 2000: Who should teach?* Available: (http://www.edweek.org/sreports/qc00/).

Foshay, R. (2000). *Instructional models: Four ways to integrate PLATO into the classroom.* (Technical Paper No. 6). Edina, MN: TRO Learning.

Fuhrman, S.H. (1994). *Challenges in systemic education reform.* (CPRE Policy Brief.) Philadelphia, PA: Consortium for Policy Research in Education.

Goetz, M.E., Floden, R.E., and O'Day, J. (1996, October). Systemic reform. In *Studies of education reform (3 vols.).* Washington, DC: U.S. Department of Education, Office of Educational Research and Improvement. Available: (http://www.ed.gov/pubs/SER/SysReform/).

Goldman, S.R. (2001). Professional development in a digital age. In D. Boesel (Ed.), *Continuing professional development* (pp. 117-136). Washington, DC: U.S. Department of Education, National Library of Education.

Haertel, G., and Means, B. (2000). *Building a foundation for a decade of rigorous, systematic educational technology research.* Available: (http://www.sri.com/policy/designkt/found.html). [To appear as two volumes with Teachers College Press in 2003.]

Hagel, J., and Armstrong, A.G. (1997). *Net gain: Expanding markets through virtual communities.* Cambridge, MA: Harvard Business School Press.

Harvard Graduate School of Education. (in press). Scaling Up Success: Lessons Learned from Technology-based Educational Innovation. Proceedings from a conference, March 20-21, 2003. Hoboken, NJ: Jossey-Bass. Paper abstracts available at http://www.gse.harvard.edu/scalingup/.

Hattie, J.A., Biggs, J., and Purdie, N. (1996). Effects of learning skills interventions on student learning: A meta-analysis. *Review of Research in Education, 66,* 99-136.

Haycock, K. (1998). Good teaching matters: How well-qualified teachers can close the gap. *Thinking K-16, 3*(2), 1-16. Available: (http://www.edtrust.org/main/main/reports.asp).

Honey, M., Culp, K.M., and Carrigg, R. (1999). *Perspectives on technology and education research: Lessons from the past and present.* New York: Center for Children and Technology.

Hoppe, U., Minrad, M., and Kinshuk, H. (2002). (Eds.). *Proceedings of the first IEEE international workshop on wireless and mobile technologies in education (WMTE'02),* August 29-30. Växjö, Sweden. New York: IEEE Press.

International Society for Teachers in Education. (1999). *National educational technology standards for students—Connecting curriculum and technology.* Eugene, OR: Author.

Kaput, J., and Hegedus, S. (2002). *Exploiting classroom connectivity by aggregating student constructions to create new learning opportunities.* Paper presented at the 26th Conference of the International Group for the Psychology of Mathematics Education, July 21-26, Norwich, UK.

Kaput, J., Noss, R., and Hoyles, C. (2001). Developing new notations for a learnable mathematics in the computational era. In L.D. English (Ed.), *The handbook of international research in mathematics* (pp. 51-73). London: Kluwer.

Kim, A. J. (2000). *Community building on the Web: Secret strategies for successful online communities.* Berkeley, CA: Peachpit Press.

Kintsch, E., Steinhart, D., Stahl, G., LSA Research Group, Matthews, C., and Lamb, R. (2000). Developing summarization skills through the use of LSA-based feedback. *Interactive Learning Environments, 8*(2), 87-109.

Knapp, M.S. (1997). Between systemic reforms and the mathematics and science classroom: The dynamics of innovation, implementation, and professional learning. *Review of Educational Research, 67*(2).

Kostoff, R.N., and Schaller, R.R. (2001). Science and technology roadmaps. *IEEE Transactions of Engineering Management, 48*(2), 132-143.

Linn, M., Davis, E., and Bell, P. (in press). (Eds.). *Internet environments for science education.* Mahwah, NJ: Erlbaum.

Mann, D., Shakeshaft, C., Becker, J., and Kottkamp, R. (1998). *West Virginia story: Achievement gains from a statewide comprehensive instructional technology program.* Santa Monica, CA: Milken Exchange on Educational Technology.

Means, B., Blando, J., Olson, K., Middleton, T., Morocco, C., Remz, A., and Zorfass, J. (1993). *Using technology to support education reform.* Washington, DC: U.S. Department of Education. Available: (http://www.ed.gov/pubs/EdReformStudies/TechReforms/).

Means, B., and Penuel, B. (in press). In *Harvard Graduate School of Education, scaling up success: Lessons learned from technology-based educational innovation. Proceedings from a conference, March 20-21, 2003.* Hoboken, NJ: Jossey-Bass.

Milken Family Foundation. (1999, September). *Survey of technology in the schools; Preliminary tables.* Santa Monica, CA. Available: (http://www.mff.org/edtech/).

Minstrell, J. (2000). Student thinking and related assessment: Creating a fact-based learning environment. In National Research Council, *Grading the nation's report card: Research from the evaluation of NAEP* (pp. 44-73). Committee on the Evaluation of National and State Assessments of Educational Progress. N.S. Raju, J.W. Pellegrino, M.W. Bertenthal, K.J. Mitchell, and L.R. Jones (Eds.). Commission on Behavioral and Social Sciences and Education. Washington, DC: National Academy Press.

Mislevy, R.J., Steinberg, L.S., and Almond, R.G. (2003). Integrating substantive and statistical arguments in educational assessment. *Measurement: Interdisciplinary Research and Perspectives, 1*(1).

Murphy, R.F., Penuel, W.R., Means, B., Korbak, C., Whaley, A., and Allen, J.E. (2002, February). *E-DESK: A review of recent evidence on the effectiveness of discrete educational software.* (SRI Project 11063). Menlo Park, CA: SRI International.

National Association of State Boards of Education. (2001). *Any time, any place, any path, any pace: Taking the lead on e-learning policy.* Available: (http://www.nasbe.org/e_learning.html).

National Commission on Mathematics and Science Teaching for the 21st Century. (2000). *Before it's too late: A report to the nation from the National Commission on Mathematics and Science Teaching for the 21st Century.* Washington, DC: U.S.

Department of Education. Available: (http://www.ed.gov/americacounts/glenn/toc.html).

National Commission on Teaching and America's Future. (1996). *What matters most: Teaching for America's future.* New York: Author. Available: (http://www.nctaf.org/publications/index.html).

National Research Council. (1997). *Developing a digital national library for undergraduate science, mathematics, engineering and technology education: Report of a workshop.* Center for Science, Mathematics, and Engineering Education, Computer Science and Telecommunications Board. Washington, DC: National Academy Press. Available: (http://books.nap.edu/books/0309059771/html/index.html).

National Research Council. (1998). *Fostering research on the economic and social impacts of information technology: Report of a workshop.* Steering Committee on Research Opportunities Relating to Economic and Social Impacts of Computing and Communications, Computer Science and Telecommunications Board, Commission on Physical Sciences, Mathematics, and Applications. Washington, DC: National Academy Press. Available: (http://books.nap.edu/books/030906032X/html/index.html).

National Research Council. (1999a). *Being fluent with information technology.* Committee on Information Technology Literacy, Computer Science and Telecommunications Board, Commission on Physical Sciences, Mathematics, and Applications. Washington, DC: National Academy Press. Available: (http://books.nap.edu/books/030906399X/html/index.html).

National Research Council. (1999b). *How people learn: Bridging research and practice.* Committee on Learning Research and Educational Practice. M.S. Donovan, J.D. Bransford, and J.W. Pellegrino (Eds.). Washington, DC: National Academy Press. Available: (http://books.nap.edu/books/0309065364/html/index.html).

National Research Council. (1999c). *Improving student learning: A strategic plan for education research and its utilization.* Committee on a Feasibility Study for a Strategic Research Program, Commission on Behavioral and Social Sciences and Education. Washington, DC: National Academy Press. Available: (http://books.nap.edu/books/0309064899/html/index.html).

National Research Council. (2000). *How people learn: Mind, brain, experience and school, Expanded edition.* Committee on Developments in the Science of Learning and Committee on Learning Research and Educational Practice. J.D. Bransford, A. Brown, and R. Cocking, (Eds.). Commission on Behavioral and Social Sciences and Education. Washington, DC: National Academy Press. Available: (http://books.nap.edu/books/0309070368/html/index.html).

National Research Council. (2001a). *Building a workforce for the information economy.* Committee on Workforce Needs in Information Technology. Board on Testing and Assessment; Board on Science, Technology, and Economic Policy; Office of Scientific and Engineering Personnel. Computer Science and Telecommunications Board. Washington, DC: National Academy Press. Available: (http://books.nap.edu/books/0309069939/html/index.html).

National Research Council. (2001b). *Knowing what students know: The science and design of educational assessment.* Committee on the Foundations of Assessment. J. Pellegrino, N. Chudowsky, and R. Glaser (Eds). Board on Testing and Assessment, Center for Education, Division of Behavioral and Social Sciences

and Education. Washington, DC: National Academy Press. Available: (http://books.nap.edu/books/0309072727/html/index.html).
National Research Council. (2002a). *Enhancing undergraduate learning with information technology: A workshop summary*. M. Hilton (Ed.), Center for Education, Division of Behavioral and Social Sciences and Education. Washington, DC: The National Academies Press. Available: (http://books.nap.edu/books/0309082781/html/index.html).
National Research Council. (2002b). *Improving learning with information technology: Report of a workshop*. Steering Committee on Improving Learning with Information Technology. G.E. Pritchard (Ed.). Center for Education, Division of Behavioral and Social Sciences and Education. Washington, DC: The National Academies Press. Available: (http://books.nap.edu/books/030908413X/html/index.html).
National Research Council. (2002c). *Preparing for the revolution: Information technology and the future of the research university*. Panel on the Impact of Information Technology on the Future of the Research University, Policy and Global Affairs. Washington, DC: The National Academies Press. Available: (http://books.nap.edu/books/030908640X/html/index.html).
National Research Council. (2003). *Strategic education research partnership*. Committee on a Strategic Education Research Partnership. M.S. Donovan, A.K. Wigdor, and C.E. Snow (Eds.). Division of Behavioral and Social Sciences and Education. Washington, DC: The National Academies Press. Available: (http://www.nap.edu/books/0309088798/html/).
National Science Foundation. (2002). *Research and development in industry: 1999*. (NSF 02-312, Project Officer and Principal Author, R.M. Wolfe). Arlington, VA: Division of Science Resources Statistics. Available: (http://www.nsf.gov/sbe/srs/nsf02312/pdfstart.htm).
National Science Foundation. (2003). *Revolutionary science and engineering through cyberinfrastructure: Report of the National Science Foundation Blue-Ribbon Advisory Panel on Cyberinfrastructure*. Arlington, VA: Author.
O'Neil, H.R. Jr. (2003). *Technology applications in education: A learning view*. Mahwah, NJ: Erlbaum.
Pea, R.D. (2002). Learning science through collaborative visualization over the Internet. In N. Ringertz (Ed.), *Nobel Symposium: Virtual museums and public understanding of science and culture*. Stockholm, Sweden: Nobel Academy Press.
Pea, R.D., Tinker, R., Linn, M., Means, B., Bransford, J., Roschelle, J., Hsi, S., Brophy, S., and Songer, N. (1999). Toward a learning technologies knowledge network. *Educational Technology Research and Development, 47*, 19-38.
Perry, G., and Talley, S. (2001). Online video case studies and teacher education: A new tool for pre-service teacher education. *Journal of Computing in Teacher Education, 17*(4), 6-31.
Phaal, R., Farrukh, C., and Probert, D. (2001, November 14). *Technology roadmapping: Linking technology resources to business objectives*. Cambridge, UK: Center for Technology Management, University of Cambridge.

President's Committee of Advisors on Science and Technology (PCAST), Panel on Educational Technology. (1997, March). *Report to the President on the use of technology to strengthen K-12 education in the United States.* Available: (http://www.whitehouse.gov/WH/EOP/OSTP/NSTC/PCAST/k-12ed.html).

President's Information Technology Advisory Committee (PITAC). (1999, February). *Information technology research: Investing in our future.* Available: (http://www.hpcc.gov/ac/report/).

President's Information Technology Advisory Committee (PITAC). (2001, February). *Using information technology to change the way we learn.* S.L. Graham and A.J. Viterbi (Chairs). Panel on Transforming the Way We Learn. Available: (http://www.hpcc.gov/pubs/pitac/index.html).

Reeves, B., and Nass, C. (1996). *The media equation: How people treat computers, television, and new media like real people and places.* New York: Cambridge University Press.

Roschelle, J., and Pea, R.D. (2002). A walk on the WILD side: How wireless handhelds may change computer-supported collaborative learning. *The International Journal of Cognition and Technology, 1*(1), 145-168.

Roschelle, J., Pea, R., Hoadley, C., Gordin, D., and Means, B. (2001). Changing how and what children learn in school with collaborative cognitive technologies. In M. Shields (Ed.), *The future of children* (Special Issue, Children and Computer Technology, published by the David and Lucille Packard Foundation, Los Altos, CA), *10*(2), 76-101.

Salvucci, D.D., and Anderson, J.R. (2000, April). Intelligent gaze-added interfaces. *Proceedings of the SIGCHI conference on human factors in computing systems,* (273-280), The Hague, The Netherlands.

Sandholtz, J., Ringstaff, C., and Dwyer, D. (1997). *Teaching with technology: Creating student-centered classrooms.* New York: Teachers College Press.

Schaller, R. (1999, March). *Technology roadmaps: Implications for innovation, strategy, and policy.* (Ph.D. dissertation proposal.) Fairfax, VA: George Mason University. Available: (http://mason.gmu.edu/~rschalle/rdmprop.html).

Schlager, M.S., Fusco, J., and Schank, P. (2002). Evolution of an on-line education community of practice. In A. Renninger and W. Shumar (Eds.). *Building virtual communities: Learning and change in cyberspace* (pp. 129-159). New York: Cambridge University Press.

Seely Brown, J., and Duguid, P. (2002). *The social life of information.* Cambridge, MA: Harvard Business School Press.

Shields, P.M., March, J., and Adelman, N. (1997). *Evaluation of the National Science Foundation's Statewide Systemic Initiatives (SSI) Program: The SSI's impacts on classroom practice.* Arlington, VA: National Science Foundation.

Shulman, J.H. (1992). (Ed.). *Case methods in teacher education.* New York: Teachers College Press.

Smith, M.S., and O'Day, J. (1991). Systemic school reform. In S.H. Fuhrman and B. Malen (Eds.), *The politics of curriculum and testing: 1990 yearbook of the Politics of Education Association* (pp. 233-267). London and Washington, DC: Falmer Press.

Snyder, T. (2000). *Outside evaluation of LemonLINK technology innovation challenge grant, evaluation year 2000*. U.S. Department of Education Grant R303A970098-01A, Edward Snyder and Associates.

Stokes, D.E. (1999). *Pasteur's Quadrant: Basic science and technological innovation*. Washington, DC: Brookings Institution Press.

U.S. Department of Energy. (2000, July). *Applying science and technology roadmapping in environmental management*. Washington, DC: Office of Environmental Management. Available: (http://emi-web.inel.gov/roadmap/guide.pdf).

Waxman, H.C., Connell, M.L., and Gray, J. (2002). *A quantitative synthesis of recent research on the effects of teaching and learning with technology on student outcomes*. Naperville, IL: North Central Regional Educational Laboratory.

Web-Based Education Commission. (2000). *The power of the Internet for learning: Final report of the Web-Based Education Commission*. Available: (http://www.ed.gov/offices/AC/WBEC/FinalReport/).

Appendix A

Reflections and Next Steps

Members of the Committee on Improving Learning with Information Technology were active participants in the January 2003 workshop, which involved exploration of the themes identified in the earlier roadmapping exercise: (1) integrating cheap, fast, robust computers into instruction for every student in the United States and (2) combining advances in the science of learning with IT capabilities to improve student learning. The workshop included a discussion of the types of activities that would be useful to pursue in the future to these ends. This Appendix presents personal statements by individual committee members on the issues raised by the 2003 workshop, as well as all the committee's activities, regarding next steps to encourage the effective use of information technology in K-12 education.

PUTTING HIGH-QUALITY CONTENT ON THE WEB AVAILABLE FREE TO ALL

Louis Pugliese and Marshall S. Smith

The purpose of this effort would be to provide the opportunity for all to easily access effectively free, high-quality, reusable digitized academic content. This includes library collections, courses, courseware, learning objects, public television shows, journals, books, art, music, and historical archives. In a recent meeting held to consider open content and its implication for developing nations, UNESCO's deputy assistant director general for communication and information stated (UNESCO, 2002):

> Knowledge has become a principal force of social transformation. Knowledge-based and -led development holds the promise that many of the problems confronting human societies could be significantly alleviated if only the requisite information and expertise were systematically and equitably employed and shared.

The Internet opens the possibility of equalizing access throughout the world to great slices of knowledge—to inhabitants of the smallest village in Africa, to citizens of the poorest cities in developing nations, and to recent Mexican immigrants in the United States.

Access to high-quality educational content is varied. Students and instructors in Berkeley or Swarthmore do not have easy access to many library collections at Harvard or to the way that a leading physicist at the Massachusetts Institute of Technology (MIT) structures her graduate seminar. Such content is far less accessible in nonelite colleges and universities throughout the United States and institutions in almost all developing nations. Similar disparities in access occur among K-12 schools in the United States. Moreover, much of the educational content now available through technology at the K-12 and postsecondary level is of poor educational quality, difficult to access, or too expensive for many to afford.

Several recent changes have opened the door to a more general strategy for improving access for all to high-quality content. These changes include the bursting of the dot.com bubble, which convinced many that it was not easy to make money on the web, the steps taken by many to place collections of educational materials on the web, and the giant leap taken by MIT to make all of its courseware available to all on the web for free in perpetuity.[1] A number of studies are currently being carried out to investigate the use and effects of the MIT initiative. If high-quality content and materials (courses, modules, learning objects, library collections, etc.) were available on the web and open to all for use and reuse, some of the gap in access to knowledge could, in theory, be overcome. In fact, a number of universities and others have set off down the road of attempting to make substantial bodies of content available in ways that have never been available in the past.

One project systematically backs up the entire World Wide Web six times a year, archives the information, and makes it publicly available at www.archive.org. Carnegie Mellon is developing a suite of stand-alone academic courses that use a cognitive tutor approach, based on current cognitive science.[2] The courses will be free to all on the web. In addition,

---

[1] See http://www.ocw.mit.edu.
[2] See http://www.cmu.edu/oli/.

some university libraries have made digitized collections of their materials open to all on the web.

There are also examples of projects that make materials available on the web at very low cost, with the money collected for use applied to sustaining the collections. JSTORE[3] and ArtSTORE are two such efforts, the first providing at low cost copies of journals and the second making available digitized art collections. The Mellon Foundation has been very active in funding this work.

The opportunity to stimulate such efforts rests, in part, on the premise that many nonprofit and government organizations, including libraries, museums, and universities, see their primary role as developing and transmitting knowledge and that, when given the opportunity to provide this knowledge free to a worldwide audience, they will do so, unless it interferes with their other responsibilities.

The challenges in creating a *useful* Internet library of free materials are many. At the forefront is to provide ways for people to screen for quality, so that they have ways of sorting through the information. The quality issue intersects with the theoretical and practical issues in the organization and structure of the materials taken one set at a time, whether they are courses, learning objects, library collections, or interactive symposiums. This form of "library" could grow like Topsy—but what kind of internal mechanism will keep it coherent, much like a "complex adaptive system" in biology? Only then can it become a commons that enhances learning and creativity (Lessig, 2001).[4] A second set of issues includes technical, business, and legal barriers, such as bandwidth and interoperability, business models for sustainability, and intellectual property issues. A third set involves making the materials as helpful and useful as possible to as many people who now do not have access as possible. For use around the world, this will require creating translations as well as research that provides a better understanding of how to stimulate the effective use of such materials.

A PULL LEARNING PARADIGM

David Vogt

The single best opportunity to improve learning with the emerging generation of information technologies is to finally enable individuals to "own" their lifelong learning experience.

---

[3] See http://www.jstore.org.
[4] See http://creativecommons.org.

None of us has ever truly and tangibly owned our learning. Consider the ownership documents. In grade school our report cards are loaned to us for brief periods of time; we share them with parents and possibly friends as proud or shameful avatars of us. In college we ask for copies of our transcripts. As workers our development is tracked somewhere in human resources files. Even as adult learners, the best we can expect is for our accomplishment to be signified by piece of paper, as if a certificate were the deed to an ephemeral learning landscape somewhere. The only token of ownership entirely in our hands is our resume or curriculum vitae. We create these and use them to represent our abilities, but they are at best grainy and ambiguously legitimate snapshots of what we know and can do.

Also consider the experience. Great teachers consistently attribute their success to granting some part of learning ownership to their students. We use terms like self-directed and learner-centered to describe our intent. We showcase models of autonomous adventure and peer exploration in problem-based learning. But we never actually give up ownership. Even in the best classrooms, students own only moments. The class ends, the school closes for the day, and the fleeting fiction is done. We expect that from occasionally allowing students to work the fields of knowledge, a delusion of land ownership will blossom, motivating them to improve that land for life. It won't happen.

The essence of the problem is that education—institutionally and technologically—has always been served, not sought. The learning industry is all push. Education has traditionally been the value-added and source-controlled distribution of knowledge and skills. In the information age, however, education itself is rapidly becoming a commodity. The old business model will soon be broken. The new value-adds will be driven by new media technologies and will balance push with pull. This is inevitable, an inescapable consequence of both the capabilities of the new technologies and the requirements of the marketplace.

The innovative applications of technology considered by the committee have all been oriented to improving the established Push Paradigm. Learning objects, content repositories, distribution networks, interoperability frameworks, adaptive learning flow algorithms, embedded assessment technologies, international accountability systems, learning management systems, etc., all enhance push. We're building a vast vending machine. Countless researchers and companies around the world are building different parts of that machine. It will work. It will become essential to learning. The only problem is that, as a commodity server, the machine will quickly learn to operate without overhead: it will be painful finding profit from the parts. There can only be so many learning management systems, for example. There are already too many. The real opportunity—commercially and educationally—is not the machine itself, but *because* of it. The top-down, push-dominated machine is exactly what is necessary to feed complementary pull technologies allowing individuals, from the bottom-up, to own, construct, and amplify their own learning experiences. The operative question then becomes, "How will my educational, career, and lifestyle goals, interpreted through the dynamic social contexts of my peers, community, and culture, determine what items I decide to select from this machine?"

Pull technologies aren't about customization, personalization, or customer relationship management. These are still forces of the push universe. Pull will be realized as a set of applications and services providing individual learners with actionable authority and versatility in the management of their lifelong learning experience. To give dimension to the Pull Learning Paradigm, consider the following scenario:

> Imagine owning a diagram that describes everything you know. Each pixel connects to courses, competencies, accomplishments, and knowledge acquired somewhere in your overall formal and informal learning history. It is a dynamic self-portrait, a visualization of who you are, with learning pathways toward who you might be some day. Use it to capture new learning experiences and shop for more. Compare your self-portrait with those of friends and communities to calibrate your differentiated identity and belongingness. Open it to potential employers to quantify your talents. Compile it with those of colleagues to bid effectively on work. Improve yourself as you wish, adorn yourself according to fashion, and market yourself as you may. Most of all, own this image as well as your reflection in the mirror—it is you and yours.

While deliberately general, this pull scenario clearly requires push. The appetite will be whetted by the vending machine. The obvious extension to this analogy is that fast food makes a poor diet: the market will also be driven to deliver more sophisticated learning experiences according to increasingly discerning tastes. Current learning providers will be challenged to compete. My organization and others are developing Pull Learning Paradigm technologies designed for such individually and socially driven pull dynamics.

Teaching and learning are among the most complex social phenomena humanity has evolved. Revolutions are therefore unlikely. Yet no revolution is required to realize the pull paradigm. The education system has been push-dominated only because there has been no mechanism within which pull could operate. The networked digitization of push has changed that. While the transition will be difficult for most institutions, it is simply a healthy balancing of push and pull. The recent transitions of the music industry are instructive. The "Napsterization" of education will be different, but it will just as inevitably and irreversibly install a push-pull dynamic in learning.

The committee was looking for a transformation of learning with information technologies. The hidden opportunity will be to enable learners to transform themselves. Pull technologies offer a very personal mediation of the mind.

A VISION FOR LENS CENTERS: LEARNING EXPEDITIONS IN NETWORKED SYSTEMS FOR 21ST CENTURY LEARNING[5]

Roy Pea and Edward Lazowska

Two broad classes of test beds are essential to inform the effective and broad-scale use of technology innovations in learning and teaching. Each can be conducted by centers that involve learning science and technology researchers, K-12 schools and stakeholders, and industries that are involved in creating the technologies used for learning and education (including hardware, software, publishing, and services). We refer to these centers as LENS centers (Learning Expeditions in Networked Systems for 21st Century Learning).

Because of their differential nature, these two classes of test beds have quite different purposes and incentives for sector participation, and they are thus likely be productively defined, funded, conducted, studied, and managed in different ways. In an important sense, the two types of test beds map onto the two transformations that the committee workshop has characterized.

The first type of test bed, the LENS "test-beds of today," take for granted the essential nature of a 1:1 computer-to-student ratio, Internet connectivity at DSL or better access speeds, teacher preparation for effective uses of technology that utilize such access, and a sufficient base of curriculum content and use of assessments that will enable both research and accountability metrics aligned with current educational standards.

---

[5]The LENS concept and acronym were developed by Roy Pea and Nora Sabelli, with input from Steve Rappoport, and some of the topics suggested here for LENS centers were developed during planning discussions to consider coordinate efforts to advance effective uses of technologies in K-12 education that were hosted by University Corporation for Advanced Internet Development (UCAID). They included participants from Advanced Network and Services, Cisco Systems, CoSN, EduCause, EDC's Center for Children and Technology, IBM, Internet-2, ISTE, League for Innovation in the Community College, MOREnet, NEA, NSBA, Nortel Networks, NoX GigaPop, Pacific Northwest GigaPop, Quilt, Qwest, SRI International, and TERC. We thank that group for seeding these thoughts on LENS for 21st century learning.

The primary role for this type of test bed is to illustrate near-term adoptable approaches for achieving the necessary condition of access to computing and communications by learners and teachers. Once developed, the promise is that what is learned from establishing what we call "test beds of today" could be emulated in other districts, cities, or states with tested technologies available now in the marketplace and be responsive to accountability metrics already in place.

The second type of test bed, the LENS "test beds of tomorrow," focuses instead on the risky unknown—on *transformational innovations for the future of learning*. The remainder of our essay focuses on such LENS test beds of tomorrow. Like work funded by the Defense Advanced Research Projects Agency in the 1960s, which led to many of the core technology innovations we take for granted today (President's Information Technology Advisory Committee, 1999), the target is radical improvements that aim for orders of magnitude possible improvements. These test beds would demonstrate feasibility and early-stage potentialities of substantively new tools, content, and pedagogies that leverage information and communication technology advances and learning science and technology knowledge at the cutting edge of what is possible. To be ready for a future world we need to explore it, as the 1999 President's Information Technology Advisory Committee report argued with its Lewis and Clark imagery of expeditions at a frontier of knowledge and life experiences transformed by technologies. We need to live in specifically created possible futures as pioneering scouts, reporting on what life is like in such possible futures. Someday the most viable LENS developments might find their way—partnerships and sustainability partners willing—into test beds of today but at a time 7-15 years or more into the future, when they may become woven into the fabric of tomorrow's societal learning systems.

We first sketch out the rationale for why LENS test beds would fill an essential need in the field today and why center structures make sense as a way to plan and study LENS test beds. We then focus on the distinctive purposes and incentives for participation in LENS centers, sketch out some exemplary LENS test bed topics of tomorrow for illustrative purposes, and then close by considering organizational aspects of the enterprise we believe would take advantage of the opportunity space for LENS centers.

Rationale

Alike in some respects (and different in others) to the pharmaceutical industry, the K-12 learning technologies world needs a pipeline, for both "push" and "pull" technologies, as David Vogt argues in his reflective essay. And research plays different roles at each stage of that pipeline, from innovative design to clinical trials, with drug discovery a crucial early-stage activity. The current policy fervor, given the No Child Left Behind Act, for randomized clinical trials as a primary model for providing scientifically based research for educational interventions does not in itself yield the innovations and programs worth devoting research funds to—we also need early-stage pilots, design research, IT-based curricula, and other forms of inquiry that are guided by science in their own right. As workshop speaker Robert Tinker noted, the Math-Science Partnership programs jointly defined by the National Science Foundation and the U.S. Department of Education, the NSF-funded Centers for Learning and Teaching, and the Department of Education's regional labs are very focused on the scaling stages of standards-focused and promising educational programs and in the aggregate cost U.S. taxpayers over several hundred million dollars per year. But these efforts will not create the innovative platforms, tools, IT-based curricula, or systemic frameworks that will be needed to take the educational enterprise supported by emerging technologies to progressive next levels.

LENS test beds of the future, organized and conducted by centers that are funded as public-private partnerships, will bring together the appropriate leadership alliances, knowledge, and communities for networking their learning and expertise and for supporting the design and conduct of new learning expeditions. No stakeholder sector alone can make the needed progress, and all have expertise to offer. LENS centers would seek to achieve "reciprocity of influence" among their stakeholders, including K-20 educators and institutions, researchers in the sciences of learning and uses of educational technologies, subject matter experts, advanced telecommunications professionals, schools of education, and industry.

Another factor contributes to the need for LENS partnership expeditions and the centers to plan, conduct, and operate them. Changes in information and computing technologies are proceeding at such a rapid pace that it will take the talented engagements of the education, research, and technology industries to forge the visions and innovations in tools, environments, and instructional practices that build on and advance the sciences and contexts of learning, teaching, and education. We worry that K-12, learning science, and the information and communication technology industry will become increasingly decoupled in their central practices without express attention to strongly supporting their convergence through LENS partnerships.

Topics for LENS Test Beds of the Future

LENS test beds might be focused on a broad range of topics of central importance for exploration and investigations concerning the future of technology-supported learning and education in society, and they may leverage and advance any configuration of emerging technologies and learning sciences research. Such expeditions will characterize kinds of demonstrable outcomes and how processes of learning through the expeditions will be documented, so that there could be demand-side interest in making these possible futures actual futures for learning with technology. Ideally, LENS expeditions would be both systemic in design and more than local in nature. By systemic we mean that they would simultaneously investigate transformed but aligned curricula, instruction, assessments, teacher learning, and connections to home and community in the future models they create and study. The following examples are provided by way of illustration as possibilities for a flagship series of LENS test beds of the future:

- Developing teacher professional development networks that integrally use digital video to share exemplary practices, reflect and advise one another, and enable distributed mentoring in a GRID-supported digital video collaboratory for teacher learning.
- Tackling the integration of advanced speech recognition, translation, and literacy development tools to make English-language learning readily accessible for all K-12 learners who are not native English speakers.
- Exploring novel uses of haptic and model-driven tele-immersive environments for learning how complex systems work in the biological and physical sciences.
- Creating learning environments and pedagogies that educate learners in approaches that foster "thinking with data" that have been collected and used in the physical and social sciences (e.g., earth and environmental sciences; digital sky; census records) and other public resources (including earth- and space-based scientific instrumentation).
- Learning high-stakes knowledge and skills in significant measure through on-line multiplayer interactive gaming that leverages engagement, motivation, and social networking, perhaps using wireless cell phone/PDA/computer platforms for the test bed and novel networks, such as peer-to-peer and mobile ad hoc networking, not only a carrier-based client-server model.
- Uses of location-aware computing to integrate learning in and out of school. For example, learning expeditions need to be developed for test beds where local community learning resources have been inventoried and information stored in wireless transmitters attached to resource loca-

tions so that a learner passing by, based on their knowledge and interest profiles, triggers the transmission of that information to their PDA.

- IT-based curricula based on fundamental rethinking of what learners and teachers can know and do and in what sequence they need to do it, based on dynamic and model-based symbolic representations (e.g., for high school students—atomic physics before molecular biology; simulation-based calculus in the upper elementary grades).
- Advanced assessment methodologies intended to guide instruction and e-learning "work flow" that not only tap into data-mining of learners' interactions with technology-based learning environments but also incorporate sensing of learning-relevant emotion and brain states that can influence learning and memory.
- Taking advantage of Internet-based technologies to enable students to remotely control parameters of powerful scientific instruments, such as telescopes and electron microscopes, to enable access to research at a distance concerning developments in such scientific topics as cosmology and nanotechnology.
- Examining the prospects for remotely controlling parameters of learning technology experiments, such as making available specific tool features or structured guidance for learners, for systematic pursuit of conjectures on interactions between learning technologies and educational environments.

Incentives for Sector Participation in LENS Centers

While test beds of today will attract the interests, expertise, and resources of the three communities we consider central, there will be different reasons for these constituencies to participate in the LENS test beds of tomorrow and centers that enable them:

- Reasons for industry to participate include the following: (1) precompetitive sharing of investment risk in testing out risky concepts not yet demonstrated as to their feasibility, readiness for market, or responsiveness to present-day market conditions and "product space" awareness; (2) desire for developing early emerging market understanding from observations of first trials of new technical capabilities in real schools and other learning settings; (3) access to knowledge sharing by learning science researchers who will seek to apply their best uses of scientific understanding in the contexts of design and innovation, to the potential benefit of industry in terms of future product development; (4) leveraging federal and foundation funding involved in the researchers' prior work or test bed engagements; (5) access to teachers and graduate students who they may wish to hire as consultants or employees later. At the same time, we must recognize that economic conditions may often make sizeable industry engagement unrealistic.

·• Reasons for learning science and technology researchers to participate include the following: (1) access to cost-sharing of real value to projects they care about and could do far less effectively with federal or foundation monies alone, including (but not limited to) uses of new authoring tools and development environments, high-end servers, next-generation hardware platforms, and communication devices; (2) research internship and apprenticeship opportunities for graduate students.

• Reasons for educators to participate are many, but include the following: (1) states may want to identify and provide special support for their main "sentinel schools" where the capacities and interests are present for taking their educational practices and tools to the next level, and in which an environment of experimentation and risk is present and the new learning from LENS participation would be an attraction; (2) opportunities abound to help advance visions of where teacher professional development and student learning are headed that schools of education could contribute to and learn from.

Organization of LENS Centers

While we believe that the LENS concept has a compelling rationale and believe there are more than sufficient incentives for the diverse stakeholders in the future of learning sciences, practices, and technologies to partake in the partnerships required to achieve them, the programmatic aspects of the LENS enterprise called for requires some consideration. LENS centers would provide institutional hubs for supporting the design, development, design research, and assessment methodologies, implementation, and the communication, groupware, and knowledge management needs that arise in the LENS partnership efforts. They may include registry services for schools, research institutes and universities, industry partners, and other organizations and assistance for brokering the formation and conduct of learning expedition partnerships across stakeholder sectors. Dissemination functions for LENS centers should be much more like interactive communication sites that invite dialogues between LENS partners and staff and the interested parties than simply knowledge-sharing activities. In this manner, the partnership focus wrought by LENS centers and their affiliated test beds for inventing the future of learning could be more successfully achieved.

REASONS FOR OPTIMISM, POSSIBILITIES FOR HARDWARE AND SOFTWARE

Edward Lazowska and Roy Pea

The track record of technology in education is clear for all to see: overpromising and underdelivering. Yet at the same time, as many futurists have noted, we tend to overestimate the effects of technology in the near term and underestimate them in the long term (Seely Brown and Duguid, 2000).

In 1922, Thomas Edison said "I believe that the motion picture is destined to revolutionize our educational system and that in a few years it will supplant largely, if not entirely, the use of textbooks." Similarly grand claims were made for radio, for television, and for computers. (We leave unattributed this 1984 statement by a highly regarded computer scientist: "There won't be schools in the future . . . the computer will blow up the school.")

Why, then, should one believe that *today* information technology offers significant promise to transform teaching and learning? We see scientific, technical, and cultural reasons for optimism.

Scientifically, there have been major advances in our knowledge of how people learn. Coupling these advances in the learning sciences with corresponding advances in educational technology is a key challenge identified in this report. How can we better undergird new designs for technology-enhanced learning environments with research knowledge and continuously improve these environments through informative ongoing assessments? To take but one salient example, we know that one-on-one human tutoring that is responsive to the learner's individual knowledge and learning pace is highly effective. Unfortunately, it doesn't scale. Well-designed education technology—education technology guided by knowledge of recent advances in the learning sciences—can augment the one-teacher-to-many-students classroom experience with instruction that simulates one teacher per learner.

Technically, Moore's Law is finally paying off. Something that matters to people is doubling every 18 months! Consider the Internet as a familiar example of this sort of exponential growth. The Internet began in 1969 with four interconnected computers. It doubled away, year after year, invisible to the public at large. Then, suddenly, in the mid-1990s, it seemed to come out of nowhere to become ubiquitous as a new infrastructure for learning, business, science, entertainment, and commerce. Exponential progress in processors, memory, storage, communication, and displays is coupled with equally rapid progress in algorithms; and the convergence of these advances is driving changes in capability and in cost that are dramatically impacting what we can do. As an example, handwriting recognition and speech recognition have made remarkable strides in the past few years. Simulation and visualization have joined theory and experiment as fundamental approaches to the practice of science; and they are beginning to impact the classroom, making the inaccessible accessible by allowing students to explore phenomena that they could not approach in the real world. Peer-to-peer schemes for rich media-sharing challenge the publishing world and digital rights management but hold great potential for educational use. And another way in which this technology is truly different from the filmstrips, radio, and television of the past is that it is a metarepresentational technology—providing a new digital medium in which one can express and connect all previous media from video, to music, to text, graphics, photography, animations, and beyond. For example, today's Google search on the World Wide Web spans over 3 billion web pages and 425 million images.

Socially, there is clear recognition that teaching and learning must be the focus, not technology. Networks and the web connect us, fostering exploration, interaction, and connectivity—communities of teachers and learners. Finally, "digital kids" are ready, calling out for learning environments that tap their new forms of digital fluency and screen literacies.

For all of these reasons, we believe that an extraordinary opportunity exists at this point in time—an opportunity that we must seize, for the sake of our children.

REFLECTIONS ON TEACHING AND TEACHERS IN THE LEMONLINK ENVIRONMENT

Barbara Allen

New classroom technologies available today have the potential to radically transform education as we know it. Successful learning no longer needs to depend on the random good fortune of always being assigned to the classes of master teachers who are both content experts and skilled learning facilitators. Instead, high-quality instruction in almost any given subject can be made available to any student of any age and any background. Students in a well-run "networked learning community" will be able to access the best educational resources from across the globe at any time of the day and year (National Association of State Boards of Education, 2001).

As part of the committee's workshop in January 2003, Darryl LaGace and I made a presentation on the Lemon Grove School District's decade-long effort to construct a connected learning community, with the district serving as the communication hub for the entire city. At the center of this effort is the district's technology initiative. Our vision is to promote academic success by providing all Lemon Grove students and their families access to direct linkups with teachers, classroom materials, and the unlimited global resources of the Internet. Project LemonLINK has focused on connectivity and access, engaging web-based curriculum, extensive professional development, and extending educational opportunities through the home connection. The district has joined with business and government partnerships to develop a unique infrastructure that connects all schools and the city via microwave, fiber optic, and laser technologies. In these additional reflections, I focus on some of the lessons we have learned about the roles of teachers and teaching in LemonLINK-like environments.

First, equipment and access should be designed with teachers and teaching in mind. Understanding classroom anomalies is crucial in system design and deployment of the technology as well as the type and focus of the professional development necessary for effective use. Under the traditional model of file servers at the school site with multimedia computers as the user device, there is an expectation that teachers will become technical experts in order to keep the equipment on line. For example, the technology proficiency rubrics for the classroom teacher developed by California's Technology Assistance Program (CTAP2),[6] which are based on the standards for teachers included in the National Educational Technology Standards (NETS) of the International Society for Technology in Education (ISTE),[7] specify that teachers who are proficient in the operation and care of hardware should be able to allocate memory needed by applications, access and change control panels, set software preferences, make more system memory available, install software, and select and use appropriate antivirus software. This concept of technological proficiency contradicts the role of the classroom teacher as defined by the profession. The California Standards for the Teaching Profession makes no mention of teachers needing to backup files, install antivirus systems, load software programs, or keep the technology in their classrooms up and running.

The traditional model of education technology using systems and devices modeled after business creates a new and disturbing element in the classroom for most teachers. CTAP2 and ISTE NETS accurately reflect the technical expertise necessary to support education technology based

---

[6] See http://ctap2.iassessment.org.
[7] See http://cnets.iste.org.

on the traditional model of technology deployment, but they cast teachers in a sometimes ill-fitting technician role to keep classroom equipment up and running for students to use technology every day. The reality is that if equipment is not reliable and functioning regularly, it will be abandoned by teachers, with Plan B quickly being implemented. If we are serious about the expectation that *all* teachers will use the tools of technology in their instruction, then network systems and devices must allow teachers to focus on creatively embedding electronic resources into everyday use for students rather than on technical support of their classroom computers.

Second, there are a number of tools that could help manage classroom environments that are rich in technology:

- **Search engines for locating quality on-line materials.** Time is a crucial factor for teachers to embed technology into their instructional practices. Over the last few years there has been a marked increase in quality on-line resources, from subscription services to materials on the Internet. The difficulty centers on the need to find appropriate on-line materials based on grade level, reading level, subject area, and curriculum standards a critical component for districts to meet No Child Left Behind criteria. For a teacher to be expected to spend hours each night locating and evaluating resources is unrealistic. Some subscription services, such as Bigchalk's Integrated Classroom and UnitedStreaming.com's streaming video collection, have built-in search mechanisms for locating targeted resources, but a broader range of products that assist in mining electronic resources based on filters set by the teacher would contribute greatly to frequency of use.
- **Electronic methods to manage on-line materials for student use.** Traditional methods of making materials available to students are distributing paper copies of information, using the overhead projector, writing information on the whiteboard, or providing oral instructions regarding the lesson. Some teachers are attempting to save URLs to Favorites on each machine each day. These instructional management practices are cumbersome and time-consuming. Seamless methods of delivery that facilitate student access to the material greatly increase the incidence of use in daily instruction. Once the teacher has located appropriate on-line materials, an electronic method is needed for centrally organizing and delivering the materials and information to students. These can be teacher developed, such as classroom Intranet sites, district-developed instructional management tools, or commercially developed products.
- **Portal technologies.** Lemon Grove School District's technology program doesn't end with the school day. With the advancement of portal technologies, it has recently developed and introduced MyLearningPortal.com,

which allows teachers and students to access district resources and programs from home or anywhere across multiple platforms, including PCs, laptops, or thin clients—all through the web with no programs required to be loaded on the local client's device. The portal allows users to log on once and gain access to customized resources targeted to the individual user's needs. For example, a teacher working on a lesson for the next day can log on from home and access materials she has developed at school using Microsoft Office XP and modify them at home even though her personal computer does not have the program loaded locally. She can then save the file back to the district storage network, and it is available to her when she arrives at school the next day. For students opting to use locally installed applications, MYePACK allows users to upload files over the web from their home computer and save it to the district storage network or turn an assignment into the teacher, thus seamlessly linking the home and work setting for teachers and students to do their work anytime, anywhere.

- **Streaming video capabilities to take advantage of the multimedia available on the Internet.** The Digital California Project is a state-funded effort to build the necessary network infrastructure required to enable California's schools to take advantage of tomorrow's advances in network technology. The network requires that schools be connected at high speeds back to the district before they can take full advantage of the resources. Lemon Grove's wide-area network now connects schools at gigabyte speeds. Even though a thin client uses very little bandwidth to run applications, the device's local media player and browsers will take as much as we can deliver in the way of streaming video. Many streaming educational resources are now available and easy to integrate into on-line lessons. No longer does the teacher have to show a 45-minute video on the classroom VCR that all students must watch at the same time. Web-based video libraries offer indexed high-quality educational videos allowing the teacher to select short clips targeting the desired instructional information that are accessed on demand by students from any workstation as many times as needed.

Third, it is important to recognize that professional development is not an event; it is a process. According to National Educational Technology Standards for Students: Connecting Curriculum and Technology *(International Society for Teachers in Education, 1999):*

> Curriculum technology integration involves the infusion of technology as a tool to enhance the learning in a content area or multidisciplinary setting. Effective integration of technology is achieved when students are able to select technology tools to help them obtain information in a timely manner, analyze and synthesize the information, and present it professionally. The technology should become an integral part of how the classroom functions—as accessible as all other classroom tools.

In order to accomplish this mighty goal for *all* teachers and not just the "techies," issues dealing with connectivity, classroom equipment and access, technical support, and instructional management tools must be resolved. When professional development relating to instructional technology no longer has to train teachers to teach in the one-computer classroom or maintain and repair equipment, the appeal of using technology in instruction becomes more widespread in the teaching ranks. Professional development takes on an entirely different look with the focus channeled to curriculum and teaching pedagogy, areas that are very familiar to teachers.

In Lemon Grove, professional development is a process that is embedded in the culture of not only the district but every school site. We no longer "do technology." Rather, discussions, demonstrations, and learning opportunities for teachers that occur throughout the work day relating to instruction, time and classroom management, communication, individualized student learning, and assessment all involve the tools that technology provides to complete the task. Skilled administrators artfully provide "just in time" intervention for teachers who need assistance in various areas of growth as they progress to the "invention" stage of the evolution of instruction in technology-rich classrooms. Our approach is quite consistent with the findings in *Teaching with Technology: Creating Student-Centered Classrooms* (Sandholtz, Ringstaff, and Dwyer, 1997):

> In the invention stage, teachers experiment with new instructional patterns and ways of relating to students and to other teachers. As more teachers reach this stage, the whole tenor of the sites begins to change. Interdisciplinary project-based instruction, team teaching, and individually paced instruction become common. Students are busier, more active; the classrooms buzz. Students can be observed helping other students over technology hurdles and they help their teachers. Teachers adapt to the more empowered status of students. Teachers increasingly reflect on their teaching to question old patterns and to speculate about the causes behind changes they see in their students.

Finally, what are our next steps in teaching and learning? Partnering with the San Diego County Office of Education's Classroom of the Future, Lemon Grove School District will expand LemonLINK by deploying a pilot 1:1 wireless thin client tablet environment in two sixth-grade classrooms beginning in September 2003. This program will not only improve the student-to-computer ratio to 1:1 by providing portable, wireless networked computing devices to each student, but it will also challenge teachers to modify pedagogy and develop new curriculum. Wireless technology will predominate connectivity as students will be provided wireless cable modems in their home to complete the home to school connection. Building on the positive features of the thin client environment, this wireless CE.net tablet will take anytime, anywhere access to a new level. As we continue to gain understanding of technology's true potential for the teaching and learning process, we stretch our vision of what is possible. The impact on achievement through adequate access and embedded integration underscores the importance of generating solutions that enable *all* districts to affordably provide sufficient daily teacher and student access to the tools and resources of technology. It is only when this level of systemic use has been realized that we can truly evaluate the impact that technology has on the learning process and student achievement.

THE POTENTIAL FOR COLLABORATION ALREADY EXISTS WITHIN THE EDUCATIONAL COMMUNITY FABRIC

Linda S. Wilson

We intuitively know that information technology tools can serve as an improvement model of education. Case studies and models of success exist throughout this country in diverse school systems and at different grade levels. Whether preparing children for success with rudimentary skills or for an increasingly technological environment, IT tools appear to make the job of education cost-effective, cost-efficient, and equitable regardless of socioeconomic community. We also know of failed systems— failure by definition due to poor implementation, lack of technical support or teacher training, or high cost.

The goodness of such an endeavor to transform education and learning technologies is recognized. It receives quick agreement in principle. How to create an environment and effort to successfully implement this endeavor demands a change in infrastructures and assessments, and it requires research in these areas. How does the education community determine what are the infrastructures, types of assessments, and research paths to pursue, without the cost of attempting several paths and risk of failure, to achieve this common goal?

Thriving organizations, industries, and institutions are such because of the ability to improve and capability to implement such improvement systemically. Similar or competitive organizations have common tasks to analyze their current situation and to determine the best approach for improvement. All must expend resources to understand these factors before implementing change. Likewise, these organizations have elemental or functional communities within them that serve sectors of the larger enterprise. Many of these organizations use a collaborative solution. This approach to cost-effective change leverages resources for research, development, and strategic position.

The successful framework of such collaboration has elements that ensure productive partnerships—a proven improvement model, a set of existing standards, a culture ripe for change, a strong leadership element, equitable representation, financial sponsoring, and a shared strategic plan that serves as a guide for the effort. This strategy then becomes pervasive in the membership communities that make up the collaborative organization, which then serve to implement the changes required to ensure success. The implementation is an ongoing effort that requires coordination, management, and review to ensure the strategic path continues to satisfy the community at large.

An example of industry collaboration that is successful and serves as a model of best practices is International SEMATECH. Formed in 1988, this consortium originally was designed to address a national crisis of market share loss in the semiconductor industry. SEMATECH began as a U.S.-only effort and with an initial membership of 14 leading-edge U.S.-based manufacturers of integrated circuits. After ten years of success as a national effort, SEMATECH's members realized that the consortium needed to reflect the global industry and invited international participation. Acknowledged success is attributed to a focused strategy of its membership, with an equitable voice from all. Extending membership to the world's leading-edge manufacturers for precompetitive cost leveraging serves to find solutions from which the entire global industry benefits and alleviates the risk of going it alone for its members in particular. The consortium strategy is enabled by continual assessment of the industry market indicators and future technical requirements. Industries around the world now use some form of collaboration and strategic goal setting to leverage cost and effort, and many use a model similar to SEMATECH's structure.

The good news is that the nature of the education community in this country is the foundation for collaboration. The makeup of the community spans all levels required for such work—policy makers, learning scientists, education administrators, curriculum developers, educators, IT suppliers, and students. These are the leaders, the implementers, and the change agents to promote and synergize partnerships. The organizations of which they are members are the sponsors and stakeholders in the effort of improvement. Each organization has dollars already allocated for research, development, or implementation of education improvement.

Partnerships and relationships exist in the education community that can spawn the groups to work on issues for the next generation of education transformations. National organizations have specific programs and working groups populated with community teams. These groups' members represent the sectors of the education system. They have established working relationships that span function and locale. The members of associations of educators, district liaisons, industry partners for better education, curriculum suppliers, and IT industries are recognized colleagues in their fields of expertise and shared values.

As a reflection of the current environments that have thriving collaborative communities, what is lacking in the education community is a formal recognition of partnerships and of an agent to serve the collaboration effort. A possible consideration of these two elements is opportune.

First, an agent is formally recognized or newly established as the organization that serves the education community and has the wherewithal to manage the collaborative system. In addition, such an agent manages the budget structure and dollars for the effort, serving the sponsoring stakeholders that are funding members of the organization. The coordination of such an effort is departmental within an organization that can support collaboration by committees populated by members of the community at large. Thus, the agent can be part of an existing organization of which these stakeholders are members or an independent consortium of stakeholders joined specifically for the purpose of next-generation education.

Second, members of the collaborative effort for improved education have a formally recognized responsibility and assignee-ship to the effort. It is crucial their organizations support and salute this membership. Currently, the population of focus groups and committees for efforts for educational improvement are accustomed to an associative membership model—a part-time role that requires some participation biannually or quarterly. The suggested model is neither demanding nor recognized as intrusive but, in most cases, more exclusive of full-time "employed" commitments. So formal termed membership is appropriate and will serve such an effort well.

The better news is that candidates exist for both the agent organization, sponsoring partners, and as group members for the teams to collaborate and form the plan that will guide education toward the next generation system. Those individuals already serving the education community associations, focus groups, and key associate positions are likely to have the credentials and commitment to execute such an endeavor. Former or current memberships of several agencies can participate as termed assignees, as with many committee memberships now existing. Likewise, industry-education partnerships exist at all levels, from national organizations to within school districts. The ability to participate in forming the strategy for the national education model as a sponsor has intrinsic value for those engaged in the beginning. Such enticements, once identified, may spark interest in those organizations motivated to improve education in their community (whether it is their town or their nation).

The best news is that formalizing the elements needed to effect change for improving the education system takes advantage of what already exists in the education communities. Industry consortiums and collaborative partnerships are familiar models of proven value in leveraging efforts throughout the country in both the public and private sectors. It makes sense to use a model that already works and one that education associations and partnerships support. The resulting strategy for better education is ensured support and continued improvement by the same population it serves.

As part of the effort of collaboration, success depends on a focused strategy of implementation over time. For serving the effort of planning two transformations in education and learning technologies, this strategic approach could be designed to accommodate the needs of the education community to achieve the next generation of education model in this country. It would comprehend at least the needs for (1) technical support infrastructures, (2) continual and appropriate assessments, (3) curricula, and (4) continuing professional education with the extensive use of IT tools.

The nature of a strategy serving a collaborative effort made of diverse communities and systems is a guide more than a stringent policy. Each local community implements tactically, thus continuing to satisfy individual sensitivities and needs in state and district education systems. Implementation is handled by those administrators and educators in such systems. Such a guide acknowledges the flexibility to address local needs as only resident experts can, while serving the higher goal of a common national objective. Typically, such an approach is known as a roadmap.

Roadmapping has certain elements, as follows: built by recognized community members who are recognized as advisers or experts (who are equitable and inclusive members representing all sectors of the community), acknowledged as a focused guideline that identifies areas of needs and implementation, and formally ratified by both the advising members and the sponsoring partners. Roadmapping is sponsored administratively and financially by partnered leaders. Each roadmap is unique and relative to the community that forms it. In the best of circumstances, it should be designed to become the accepted guide, since it is built and ratified by representatives of that community. It could be noted that the elements for successful collaboration cited earlier are similar, if not the same. As stated earlier, many of these elements need only to be formalized and directed toward the effort of transforming education and learning technologies.

Existing partnerships and alliances in the national education community are success factors for the leadership and collaboration. Working relationships can be formalized into focus teams, and a coordinating organization of such a strategic effort can be recognized. In addition, the

IMPROVING LEARNING WITH INFORMATION TECHNOLOGY

Edward R. Dieterle II

strategy produced by such teams, which serves to continually guide the community, such as a roadmap, is critical to the effort.

In the winter of 2001, a project director of the National Research Council (NRC) contacted me with an invitation to serve on the Improving Learning with Information Technology (ILIT) committee. Prior to our conversation, I knew little about the relationship between the NRC and teachers. During the months that I have worked with the committee, I have come to learn of the NRC's interests in education and education reform. I have also come to appreciate the committee's attempt at bridging the relatively independent communities of teachers, learning scientists, and the information technology industry. It was also during my service that I made the decision to leave my chemistry classroom and begin a doctoral program in learning and teaching with the ultimate goal of working with emerging teachers. The following reflection draws on my experiences as a classroom teacher and a member of the committee and documents my transformation from a novice to an experienced user of information technology to improve student learning.

During my first two years in the classroom, the professional enculturation of balancing the professional duties with the instructional responsibilities of a teacher overwhelmed me. While computers played an important role in my personal productivity, I did not understand the potential that information technology offered my pedagogy. By my third year of teaching, I began to understand and appreciate the culture of my classroom and my school and had developed good working relationships with my department chair, immediate colleagues, and administration. As I looked for new ways to improve my teaching and my students' learning, a chance discussion with my department chair concerning the Internet changed my outlook forever.

As my department chair taught me how to effectively search the Internet for images to use in upcoming lessons, I began to value how the Internet could bring up-to-date information and images to my classroom. After finding images and pasting them into multimedia slides, I projected them to my students. My initial projection device was a 30-inch monitor the school had purchased earlier in the year. Since very few teachers in the building were interested in using the monitor, I adopted it as a permanent addition to my classroom. After sharing the multimedia slides with my classes, it became obvious that several students in the class were experienced Internet researchers. Using my Internet-savvy students as resources, I proceeded to relinquish my power to those who knew. Although I comprehended more chemistry than my students did, I became as much a student as everyone else in the class on Internet use and multimedia design. Collectively we tried to determine the properties of good slides and ways of improving poor ones. I then began transforming many of my traditional chemistry projects to include multimedia components. In addition, my students and I began collaborating via email. It was during this time that I realized how students develop different voices while in this alternative medium. Moreover, some students who were less vocal in class thrived in email discussions. Email also afforded the quick exchange of documents in our learning community.

In terms of student learning and my own teaching, I gathered four take-away ideas about multimedia development. First, the novelty of new technology is bound to excite some while intimidating others. Since I was able to highlight my own learning and imperfections in class, I believe my students were less critical of their own mistakes. Second, the multimedia collaboration encouraged students to articulate verbally their own learning. As a teacher, I became a much better educator when I knew how students were thinking and learning. This shift in teaching also led to my first vivid experience of students' zone of proximal development; that is, the increased learning potential children have while working collaboratively with more capable peers or under adult guidance and ultimately "what a child can do with assistance today she will be able to do by herself tomorrow" (Vygotsky, 1978:86-87).

Third, content is the hallmark of good work. Initially, my students were convinced that bells and whistles were necessary for great presentations and that scientific content was a secondary concern. To redirect and focus everyone, we began developing presentations in black and white with appropriate images, then added colors and effects. Fourth, for students to be effective producers of multimedia products, they need low computer-to-student ratios, fast Internet connections, and regular access. The administration and technology coordinator of my school granted my request for additional resources based on my effective usage of the technology I had and my ability to define future learning potentials.

At the start of my fourth year of teaching, I had four Internet-connected computers in my classroom. While my students and I continued to develop multimedia presentations, we came upon a major roadblock. Not everyone in class had equal access to the multimedia software outside class. It was during this time that a student introduced me to WYSIWYG editors—*what you see is what you get* web page editors whose interface is similar to that of word processors. WYSIWYGs are free, cross-platform, and do not require state-of-the-art computers.

As my students and I began learning about web page design, my teaching shifted again. Instead of developing independent projects or web pages, we developed web sites. The products of this shift became the backbone of my chemistry curriculum. Examples of units we developed include *The Virtual Periodic Table* (Dieterle and Bois, 1999), *Hurricanes Are Low Pressure and High Stress* (Dieterle and Gavin, 1999), and *Radon Raiders Inc.* (Dieterle and Bois, 2000). In each of these projects, groups of students developed web pages for the usable class web site. These lessons were developed for Maryland Public Television and drew on the teaching philosophies of *Understanding by Design* (Wiggins and McTighe, 1998), *Teaching for Understanding* (Wiske, 1998), WebQuests (Dodge, 2003), and Public Television's NTTI program (Maryland Public Television NTTI Home Page, 2003).

My students' learning and my own teaching transformed again as my maturity and innovation with information technology expanded. Reflecting on this period, I gathered three additional take-away ideas. First, web page viewing and development are possible on almost all computers. Second, students value their work when they realize it is public and meaningful. Third, web page and web site development is an ongoing and iterative process. As students continue to deepen their understandings, they have the ability to update their products, which is very different from my original one-time, individual projects.

As my knowledge of web pages grew, my ability to maintain a class web page also grew. By my last year in the classroom, my students and I had access to technologies that extended the learning experience beyond our face-to-face meetings. Besides access to daily and archived notes, laboratories, and projects, our class maintained an asynchronous discussion board where thoughts and ideas could be unpacked and explored. This particular medium allowed students to find new and powerful voices since they had time to reflect and prepare their responses before posting them. Topics discussed in this medium fostered a level of collaboration and understanding I had never experienced before. In addition, I found the class discussion board equally beneficial to traditionally low- and high-performing students.

As a classroom teacher, I cannot imagine teaching class without the information technology tools that I have become accustomed to using. Not only did they help me organize and streamline my curriculum, but they also helped me teach and learn with students in ways that I could not have previously enjoyed. In addition, my success and the success of many of my teaching peers was possible only because of the harmony between the hardware (e.g., computers and the network), software (a variety of open-ended applications), and peopleware (a supportive administration and an effective technology coordinator) in my school and county. My recommendation to fellow teachers is to start small and to use the technology that you have available to you for your own productivity. When you see the value in something that you find or produce, share it with your students and colleagues and ask them to do the same. Powerful learning media such as asynchronous discussion boards, instant messengers, and email allow students to assume different classroom roles. Those who are quiet face-to-face might find their voice on line. Just as Rome was not built in a day, expert use of information technology in classroom instruction to improve student learning does not happen overnight.

During my period with the committee, I regularly observed the appetite and potential to bring the teaching, learning scientists, and information technology industry communities together in order to improve learning with information technology. Since I have become a doctoral candidate at the Harvard Graduate School of Education, I have taken many courses that deeply explore bridging learning theory, design, practice, and policy. The successes highlighted during my first year tend to exemplify constructive and collaborative communication among the communities of teachers, learning scientists, and the information technology industry. While the success stories of these courses were small in scale, each magnified the complications and frustrations I observed while on the committee surrounding community, scale, and sustainability. Just as an individual teacher transforms himself and increases the opportunities for his students to learn by finding value in the power of the technology and by successfully bridging his microcosm of teaching, learning theories, and information technology, it is my hope that the work of the committee continues to expand the communication webs of teachers, learning scientists, and the information technology industry.

DEVELOPING, DEPLOYING, AND EVALUATING HIGH-QUALITY SOFTWARE FOR TEACHING ENGLISH TO ENGLISH LANGUAGE LEARNER STUDENTS AND FOR TUTORING AND PROVIDING PRACTICE IN READING AND MATHEMATICS FOR STUDENTS WHO NEED EXTRA SUPPORT

Marshall S. Smith

This essay focuses attention on the needs of students who are now at risk of failure, and it addresses the issues that schools are most concerned with—teaching English to non-English speakers and competence for all in reading and mathematics. The idea is not to replace teachers or require teachers to alter their practice. Instead it is to complement existing teaching by providing opportunities to students to spend more time learning and practicing the use of language and mathematics skills.

Those most in need often are not given the support and educational experiences at home and in their neighborhood that more advantaged students take for granted. Between ages 5 and 17, students are in school for less than 20 percent of their waking hours. Many low-income students enter school with vocabularies that are far smaller than average middle-income students. While they are growing up, their opportunities to practice reading and mathematics at home are substantially lower than the opportunities of middle-income students. A high percentage of Hispanic immigrants live in homes in which the predominant language is Spanish and they get no opportunity to practice speaking or listening to English. These students need the opportunity that others have to have their school experiences expanded and reinforced beyond the normal classroom. They need more time on task to have an equal opportunity (e.g., Hart and Risley, 1995; Alexander, Entwisle, and Olson, 2001).

For a variety of reasons, this is the right time to develop and test new teaching programs for these purposes. First, there is increased emphasis in the United States on providing extra educational opportunities for needy students during school and through after-school and summer programs. The general policy of extending time is reflected in the federal government's 21st century after school program, in the new requirements for Title I of the Elementary and Secondary Education Act, in state accountability laws throughout the country, and in the rise of charter schools like KIPP (Knowledge Is Power Program), which provide educational services for 10 hours a day, six days a week. Second, there are increased numbers of poor and minority families with access to computers and opportunities for using computers outside of normal school hours in schools, libraries, and youth clubs.

Third, we have learned a lot about designing instructional IT programs and about how students learn. There has been a substantial amount of applied research on how students learn most effectively using the computer. Moreover, cognitive science and technology have made it possible to provide sophisticated and very transparent (to the user) cognitive tutoring and practice on basic skills both on CDs and through the web so it is available anytime, anywhere. Computer tutoring and practice have been used for years and have been shown to be effective. In recent years we have learned large amounts about how to incorporate cognitive tutoring and smart adaptive approaches based on built-in formative assessments. But straightforward, transparent programs for low-income students and English-language learners that incorporate up-to-date knowledge about instructional design and cognitive science are not available (O'Neil, 2003; National Research Council, 2002).

Finally, new technology in voice recognition, voice generation, and language translation makes possible powerful software that provides effective tutoring and structured practice in primary and second language learning for students of all ages. The largest need for such programs is for recent immigrants from Spanish speaking and Asian language nations.

An aggressive program of design, development, and research is needed to develop effective tutoring and practice software for learning to read, language development, arithmetic, and English-language learning. The instructional software must go well beyond the existing rote, drill, and practice programs that are currently used. We have the technology and the knowledge to do this; all we need is the will.

One initial target population would be second through fifth graders in schools, extended after-school and summer school programs, libraries, clubs, and homes. Programs could be designed for stand-alone PCs and Game Boy-like play machines. Versions should be designed for students to work alone as well as for pairs and groups of students. The use of the programs and their purposes need to be very transparent.

The teaching programs should be provided free on the web for use by anyone at any time. Teacher professional development for ways of providing support for students could also be provided in linked web-based and free programs.

CHANGES IN TECHNOLOGY AND ITS APPLICATION TO LEARNING

Miriam Masullo

Technology trends are emerging faster and with increasing impact on everyday activities. On an extended time scale, the rate of growth of information technology power, performance, and corresponding improvement in price is today about 60 percent from 20 percent in the early 20th century. The fundamental technologies that have changed the world are extremely dense storage, enormous bandwidth, and faster and smaller transistors. And while we expect substantial technical and physical barriers to progress in these areas, history has shown that we always find new technologies to go beyond those that are reaching their natural limitations.

In 1965, just a few years after the first planar integrated circuit was invented in 1959, Moore predicted that the number of transistors per integrated circuit would double every 18 months. He forecast that this trend would continue through 1975, for a mere 10 years. We continue to break down barriers to Moore's Law, and today a Pentium 4 processor introduced in the year 2000 reaches more than 50 million transistors. In what has been called "disruptive technologies," we see a threat in IT progress because we cannot incorporate technologies as fast as we break the laws that govern them.

In the next 10 to 20 years, some key thresholds will be crossed. For example, it will cheaper to store images digitally, and they will be played back with higher resolution than the human eye can see. Not only will we be interacting with billions of devices, but also billions of devices will be interacting with each other. Wireless connected pervasive devices will be the dominant means of information processing and access. Environment-aware, locality-aware, and scenario-aware products will guide us, creating a digitally enhanced physical world. Indeed, at some point in time it will be hard to differentiate between physical and digital realities—both will be real in our future, the IT-enhanced world of the future.

Successful companies upgrade constantly, but that is not something we can do with schools or with policies. Home learners and private and charter schools are making fundamental changes to their IT environments that public schools cannot make. Should we hold back all school learning? Should we provide equity access to emerging technologies? Neither will work because neither is possible.

Our classrooms will exist in the IT-enhanced world of the future, unless we force them to remain in the past. Socially, future generations of students will not remain in the past, and this will create social and intellectual problems for which we may not have any solutions. Simply put, the problem for education is: How will people learn to live with these technologies if we don't find a way for people to learn with technologies?

Web technologies of the present developed over the last decade through an unprecedented burst of entrepreneurial energy and global cooperation. Competitive forces led to innovative technologies. The competitive tension and global cooperative standards that ensued created an IT climate irrelevant to education and learning. Web-standard technologies without reliance on market license fees are a by-product of business and the only benefit to education, a fragile benefit at that. The second decade of the web demonstrated that patents are a factor in the ongoing evolution of the web infrastructure. Schools, education, and learning stand to be left out of the ultimate phase of web-based IT; this is important because of the inseparable involvement of the web with telecommunications. It is unclear what will happen without effective and profoundly knowledgeable policies. We cannot afford not to know what laws to pass, but not a single member of Congress is an expert in IT. Therefore, our IT-enhanced future is in the minds of lobbyists and politics. Schools, education, and learning stand to lose out.

To guide the use of IT in K-12 education, we should agree on some core principles:

- We cannot allow politics to chart the future of our schools.
- We must explicitly define IT policy requirements for our schools.
- We must not allow schools to be second to industry in the IT future.

How do we enforce these guiding principles in a nation that is guided by a notable free enterprise system that is the envy of the world? How do we enforce these guiding principles in the midst of a global economy in which our schools stand to challenge no one in the world? Who cares what happens to our schools?

E-learning is the application of e-business technology to education and learning. It is a currently a web-enabled enterprise application, including the entire spectrum from back-end systems to front-end linkages, such as learning delivery systems, learning management, and the underlying infrastructure, including network infrastructure, middleware, storage, servers, and client systems. E-learning requires a successful evolution of *learning objects* as part of the ongoing evolution of IT.

According to industry research, customers (e.g., schools) want to be able to buy fine-grained content from multiple publishers, so that teachers can deliver personalized classes. Publishers have historically adopted proprietary standards for delivering coarse-grained, rigidly structured content; and they will need to adapt to the market requirements of the e-learning industry, which are different from traditional education markets.

Publishers strongly desire standards in this industry, but a lack of conviction that current processes will yield useful results in the short term is holding back such standards development. The emergence of an open standards-based economy for the creation, distribution, composition, and delivery of learning objects supporting digital rights management would turn this industry into the future of IT-based education; and that might be the only hope for participation of schools in the IT-enhanced future described earlier.

TECHNOLOGY AND THE ADVANCEMENT OF EDUCATIONAL ASSESSMENT

James W. Pellegrino

A theme of this workshop, as well as this committee's activities since its inception, is that extremely powerful information technologies will become as ubiquitous in educational settings as they are in other aspects of people's daily lives. They are almost certain to provoke fundamental changes in learning environments at all levels of the education system. Indeed, reports by groups such as the President's Council of Advisers on Science and Technology and the Web-Based Education Commission, as well as examples of transformations of practice such as the Lemon Grove school system, indicate that many of these changes are already occurring. Conjecture abounds about the consequences for children, teachers, policy makers, and the public, even though many of the implications of technology are beyond people's speculative capacity. A decade ago, for example, few could have predicted the sweeping effects of the Internet on education and other segments of society.

While it is always risky to predict the future, it appears clear that advances in technology will continue to impact the world of education in powerful and provocative ways. Many technology-driven advances in the design of learning environments will reshape the terrain of what is both possible and desirable in education. Advances in curriculum, instruction, assessment, and technology are likely to continue to move educational practice toward a more individualized and mastery-oriented approach to learning. This evolution will occur across the K-20 spectrum. To manage learning and instruction effectively, people will want and need to know considerably more about what has been mastered, at what level, when, and by whom. To do so we must have highly effective ways of assessing the processes and outcomes of teaching and learning.

It is frightening then to juxtapose today's educational assessment practices with the realities of today's, much less tomorrow's, technology-enabled educational practices. Much of contemporary educational assessment continues to be predicated largely on the use of highly restricted, drop-in-from-the-sky external accountability tests, administered primarily in paper-and-pencil formats. As argued in the recent NRC report *Knowing What Students Know* (National Research Council, 2001b), the knowledge base exists to put in place a more rational and educationally useful approach to assessment. Furthermore, much of what needs to be done to design and implement such assessments rests on intelligent uses of technology. The NRC report devotes an entire chapter to the opportunities afforded by technology for improving teaching and learning by improving the design and use of educational assessments.

At a very basic level, information technologies help remove many of the constraints that have limited assessment practice in the past. Among the most intriguing applications of technology are those that extend the nature of the problems that can be presented and the knowledge and cognitive processes that can be assessed. By enriching task environments through the use of multimedia, interactivity, and control over the stimulus display, it is possible to assess a much wider array of cognitive competencies than has heretofore been feasible. New capabilities enabled by technology include directly assessing problem-solving skills, making visible sequences of actions taken by learners in solving problems, and modeling and simulating complex reasoning processes. Technology also makes possible data collection on the conceptual organization of students' knowledge, as well as representations of their participation in discussions and group activities.

Another significant contribution of technology to assessment practice is in the design of systems for implementing sophisticated classroom-based formative assessment activities. Technology-based systems have been developed to support individualized instruction by extracting key features of learners' responses to sets of problems, analyzing patterns of correct and incorrect reasoning, and providing rapid and informative feedback to both student and teacher (see e.g., Kintsch et al., 2000; Minstrell, 2000; Vendlinski and Stevens, 2002).

While selected examples of innovative assessment designs and practices can be found in the research and development literature, it is also clear that much more research and development work needs to be done to understand the design principles on which they are built, to extend them to multiple areas of curriculum and instruction, and to explore the power and impact of such systems on student learning and teacher instructional practices. For further discussion of these issues see the *Knowing What Students Know* report (National Research Council, 2001b).

Assuming that such an agenda will attract adequate funding and be carefully pursued, it is important to consider the broader possibilities that might arise for educational practice and policy if and when technology-based assessment is systematically integrated into instruction across multiple curricular areas. Technology could then offer ways of creating, over time, complex streams of data about how students think and reason while engaged in important learning activities. Information for assessment purposes could be extracted from this stream and used to serve both classroom and external assessment needs. In such a world, programs of on-demand external assessment, such as state achievement tests, might not be necessary. Instead, it might be possible to extract the information needed for summative and program evaluation purposes from data about student performance continuously available both in and out of the school context.

A metaphor for such a radical shift in how one "does the business of educational assessment" exists in the world of retail outlets, ranging from small businesses to supermarkets to department stores. No longer do these businesses have to close down once or twice a year to take inventory of their stock. Rather, with the advent of automated checkouts and bar codes for all items, these enterprises have access to a continuous stream of information that can be used to monitor inventory and the flow of items.

Not only can business continue without interruption, but the information obtained is far richer, enabling businesses to monitor trends and aggregate the data into various kinds of summaries. Similarly, with new assessment technologies, schools would no longer have to interrupt the normal instructional process at various times during the year to administer external tests to students. Nor would they have to spend significant amounts of time preparing for specific external tests peripheral to the ongoing activities of teaching and learning.

Clearly, technological advances will allow for attainment of many of the goals that educators, researchers, policy makers, teachers, and parents have envisioned for assessment—namely that it serve as a viable source of information for educational improvement. When powerful technology-based instructional and assessment systems are implemented in classrooms, rich sources of information about student learning can be continuously available across wide segments of the curriculum and for individual learners over extended periods of time. This is exactly the kind of information we now lack, making it difficult to use assessment data to truly support learning.

The major issue is not whether this type of data collection and information analysis is feasible in the future. Rather, the issue is how the world of education anticipates and embraces this possibility and how it explores the resulting options for effectively using assessment information to meet the multiple purposes served by current assessments and, most important, to enhance student learning. Such an exploration of linkages between technology and assessment practices must also grapple with numerous critical issues, such as utility, practicality, cost, equity, and privacy.

It has been noted that the best way to predict the future is to invent it. Without doubt, multiple futures for educational assessment could be invented based on synergies that we know exist among information technologies and advances in the sciences of learning *and* measurement. While we are a considerable distance away from implementing the types of fully integrated systems envisioned above, there are steps that must be taken now that would put us on the path to such a future.

REFERENCES

Alexander, K.L., Entwisle, D.R., and Olson, L.S. (2001). Schools, achievement, and inequality: A seasonal perspective. *Educational Evaluation and Policy Analysis*, 23(2), 171-191.

Dieterle, E., and Bois, J. (1999). *The virtual periodic table*. Available: http://www.mpt.org/learningworks/teachers/ntti/8-12/periodictoc.shtml [February 22, 2003].

Dieterle, E., and Bois, J. (2000). *Radon Raiders, Inc.: Radon's connection to cancer WebQuest.* Available: http://www.pgcps.pg.k12.md.us/~nwest/biohealth/Lungs.htm [February 22, 2003].

Dieterle, E., and Gavin, J. (1999). *Hurricanes are low pressure and high stress!* Available: http://www.mcps.k12.md.us/mtlt/institute99/lesson_plans.html [February 22, 2003].

Dodge, B. (2003). *The WebQuest page at San Diego State University.* Available: http://webquest.sdsu.edu/webquest.html [February 22, 2003].

Hart, B., and Risley, T.R. (1995). *Meaningful differences in the everyday experience of young American children.* Baltimore, MD: Brookes.

International Society for Teachers in Education. (1999). *National educational technology standards for students: Connecting curriculum and technology.* Eugene, OR: Author.

Kintsch, E., Steinhart, D., Stahl, G., LSA Research Group, Matthews, C., and Lamb, R. (2000). Developing summarization skills through the use of LSA-based feedback. *Interactive Learning Environments, 8*(2), 87-109.

Lessig, L. (2001). *The future of ideas: The fate of the commons in a connected world.* New York: Random House.

Maryland Public Television NTTI Home Page. (2003). Available: http://www.mpt.org/learningworks/teachers/ntti/home.shtml [February 22, 2003].

Minstrell, J. (2000). Student thinking and related assessment: Creating a fact-based learning environment. In National Research Council, *Grading the nation's report card: Research from the evaluation of NAEP* (pp. 44-73). Committee on the Evaluation of National and State Assessments of Educational Progress. N.S. Raju, J.W. Pellegrino, M.W. Bertenthal, K.J. Mitchell, and L.R. Jones (Eds.). Commission on Behavioral and Social Sciences and Education. Washington, DC: National Academy Press.

National Association of State Boards of Education. (2001). *Any time, any place, any path, any pace: Taking the lead on e-learning policy.* Washington, DC: Author.

National Research Council. (2001b). *Knowing what students know: The science and design of educational assessment.* Committee on the Foundations of Assessment. J. Pellegrino, N. Chudowsky, and R.Glaser (Eds.). Board on Testing and Assessment, Center for Education, Division of Behavioral and Social Sciences and Education. Washington, DC: National Academy Press. Available: http://books.nap.edu/books/0309072727/html/index.html.

National Research Council. (2002). *Preparing for the revolution: Information technology and the future of the research university.* Panel on the Impact of Information Technology on the Future of the Research University, Policy and Global Affairs. Washington, DC: The National Academies Press. Available: http://books.nap.edu/books/030908640X/html/index.html.

O'Neil, H.R. Jr. (2003). *Technology applications in education: A learning view.* Mahwah, NJ: Erlbaum.

Sandholtz, J., Ringstaff, C., and Dwyer, D. (1997). *Teaching with technology: Creating student-centered classrooms.* New York: Teachers College Press.

Seely Brown, J., and Duguid, P. (2002). *The social life of information.* Cambridge, MA: Harvard Business School Press.

UNESCO. (2002). *Forum on the impact of open courseware for higher education in developing countries.* Paris: Author. Available: http://www.wcet.info/resources/publications/unescofinalreport.pdf.

Vendlinksi, T., and Stevens, R. (2002). A Markov model analysis of problem-solving progress and transfer. *Journal of Technology, Learning and Assessment.* 1(3).

Vygotsky, L.S. (1978). *Mind in society: The development of higher psychological processes.* Cambridge, MA: Harvard University Press.

Wiggins, G., and McTighe, J. (1998). *Understanding by design.* Alexandria: ASCD.

Wiske, M.S. (1998). (Ed.). *Teaching for understanding: Linking research with practice.* San Francisco: Jossey-Bass.

Appendix B

Key Enablers for the Two Transformations

This Appendix provides the lists of key enablers (first level entries) and descriptors and comments (second level entries) that were developed in the breakout groups of the January 20, 2003, workshop. After elaborating their candidates for key enablers, participants reviewed the lists of all four groups and voted for their top two choices for key enablers. The numbers in parentheses provide the number of votes received by each key enabler.

FIRST TRANSFORMATION

Group 1

- ❖ Demonstrable added value for teachers' work practices—integration (11)
  - ➢ Lesson preparation, assessment, credentialing, personalization, class management
  - ➢ Must be ready to hand
- ❖ Clearly defined goals, strategies, management (5)
  - ➢ Leadership capacity, integration of technology and curriculum, control, innovation management—need top-down/bottom-up interplay
  - ➢ At what level should leadership be?

- ❖ Quality of service (2)
  - ➢ Physical and intellectual accessibility, support, reliability
  - ➢ What is right level for locating support?
- ❖ Clearly defined content/use, resource discovery
  - ➢ People are buying the hardware!
  - ➢ How can content be found?
  - ➢ "It's the software, stupid!"

Group 2

- ❖ Colleges/universities need to be aligned with new challenges (9)
  - ➢ Content courses with embedded new technologies
  - ➢ Integrated curriculum for preservice education that connects letters, art, and sciences
  - ➢ Close gap between education programs and real-world needs of teachers
- ❖ Curriculum, pedagogy, and technical support must be organically linked (4)
  - ➢ The content/concept/pedagogy tied dynamically to technology in teacher's mind
- ❖ Encourage design/development process that closes gap between teacher/student and developer (2)
- ❖ Work flow efficiency must be built into educational technology—design and acquisition (2)
- ❖ Creation and adoption of common system for sharing, evaluating, and distributing teacher-created materials

Group 3

- ❖ Build case (with business and educator involvement) for risk taking with public money (6)
  - ➢ Need evidence/examples/case studies
- ❖ Assessments need to change (2)
  - ➢ Crack cycle of textbooks-to-curriculum-to-standardized tests
- ❖ Tipping points (see business case, above):
  - ➢ Make education attractive to industry (1)
  - ➢ Educators need to believe in vision, i.e., embrace technology, content need, partnership with industry
  - ➢ Cost-benefit convincing story
- ❖ Change mindset in education and business (1)
  - ➢ Need data, case studies
- ❖ Need leadership—all levels

Group 4

- Research-based body of evidence on what works (6)
  - Prove that technology enhances achievement
- Systems approach (5)
  - People and community and technology
  - Establishing education model
- Leadership and professional development, plus preservice improvements (3)
- Public acceptance of 21st century skills basis (3)

SECOND TRANSFORMATION

Group 1

- Define goals and metrics (12)
- Redesign and make effective a cycle between research, training, practice, and assessment
- Create a functioning marketplace for translating research into goods and services (3)
- Build public and policy awareness around need for the vision and roles (2)
- Carry out LENS[1] expeditions (8)
- Develop set of "middleware" tools
- Innovation portfolio[2] (1)
- Develop schools as learning organizations
- Capitalize on learner innovation

Group 2

- Promoting/clarifying "the vision"
- Research funding for:
  - Potential of new technologies to better assess process and learning
  - Ongoing formative assessment of learning for students and teachers
  - Large-scale and long-term questions
- Moving beyond paper-and-pencil assessment (1)
- Create cognitive science/IT tech parks similar to those of university/private-sector partnerships (6)
  - Teacher involvement

---

[1] See discussions by Roy Pea in Chapter 3 and in Appendix A.
[2] See discussion by Robert Tinker in Chapter 3.

- ➢ Graduate student involvement
- ➢ University/company intellectual property sharing
- ❖ Develop a metametrics of what works, build broad stakeholder consensus on metrics and hold accountable to those metrics (1)

Group 3

- ❖ Targeted test beds: proof of concept to support first transformation (12)
- ❖ Generate compelling examples (1)
- ❖ Funding (1)
- ❖ Use known success models from other communities of research
- ❖ Build constituencies
- ❖ Include reward structure like health/sciences (1)
- ❖ Practical partnerships (1)

Group 4

- ❖ Stable over time in contrast to relearning over time: hardware, software, content
- ❖ Measure added value
- ❖ Explore tax structure (1)
- ❖ R&D on formative assessments (4)
- ❖ Professional development and R&D on how students learn and assessments
  - ➢ Give incentives to learn
- ❖ Long-term implementation research
- ❖ Restructure school time to maximize learning
- ❖ Greater understanding of how to innovate/institutional support of innovation; incentives for teachers to be innovative

Appendix C

Workshop Materials

DECEMBER 2001 WORKSHOP AGENDA

Committee on Improving Learning with Information Technology

Workshop
December 11, 2001

8:30 am **Welcome, Introduction of ILIT Committee, and Project Overview**
Oak Room
Roy Pea and Wm. A. Wulf, ILIT cochairs

8:45 **Workshop Participant "Show and Tell"**

Attendees are invited to share information or a short demonstration of some exciting education technology they are familiar with (5 minute limit).

- Michael Turturice will share his experience as a first year teacher in a fully online criminal justice class that he created through and for Virtual High School <www.govhs.org>.
- Jim Minstrell will present the tools of the Diagnoser Project. Teachers use it for formative assessment in science and mathematics from grades 7-10. It is also considered a professional development tool for teachers to learn more about

content but especially to learn more about learners' thinking in science and mathematics <tutor.psych.washington.edu>.

9:30 Break

9:45 **Understanding Literacy in an Educational Context**
Tom Landauer, University of Colorado

Professor Landauer will discuss "reading to learn" literacy challenges as a contextual foundation for viewing the subsequent technology demonstrations.

Tom Landauer joined Bell Labs in 1969, where he worked in the Human Information Processing research department until the late seventies when he formed the computer-user psychology group, the first industrial human-computer interaction research laboratory. This group moved to Bellcore and changed its name and span of interest to Cognitive Science Research. A highly interactive team of computer scientists and cognitive psychologists, the group specialized in research on information retrieval, navigation and display, primarily based on empirical studies of users and the invention of computer-based solutions to their problems, as well developing methods for improving the usefulness and usability of computer-based mental work tools in general. Landauer was the group's director from 1984 to 1994. Among its major accomplishments were the development of the Latent Semantic Indexing (LSI) text retrieval method and the SuperBook text browser. Landauer was one of the principal designers of both, and of several other applications. In 1994, Landauer moved to the University of Colorado, Boulder, where he is a professor of psychology and a fellow of the Institute of Cognitive Science, an interdisciplinary combination of cognitive psychology, linguistics, computer science, education and philosophy. Landauer is a fellow of the American Association for the Advancement of Science (AAAS), the American Psychological Association and the American Psychological Society. He received his Ph.D. in psychology from Harvard.

10:15 **General Overview of Each Technology Station** (5 minute limit)
Marlene Scardamalia and Chris Teplovs, Knowledge Forum
Susan Goldman, Little Planet Literacy Series
Bernard Dodge, WebQuest

10:30 **Break and Groups of 20 Shift to View the Technology Stations**

APPENDIX C

10:45 **Three Stations Showcasing a Variety of Technologies Contributing to "Reading to Learn" Literacy Goals**

The participants will circulate among three different stations.

- Spruce Room, Station 1: **Knowledge Forum,** which allows users to create a knowledge-building community. Each community creates its own database in which to store notes, connect ideas, and tackle complex problem solving. The note-taking, searching, and organizational features of this sophisticated tool allow any type of community to build knowledge.
- Maple Room, Station 2: **Little Planet Literacy Series**, developed in collaboration with Vanderbilt University's Learning Technology Center, an interdisciplinary group involved in state of the art cognitive research on learning with technology. The series involves "Anchored Instruction," which is a multi-sensory approach. Anchored Instruction works for students with a wide variety of abilities, including those with very limited literacy skills. Students accomplish a series of tasks revolving around the context of a single story or "Anchor Story" by collaborative or individual effort. By revising the story and sharing the common knowledge of the Anchor Story, students become successful readers and writers.
- Oak Room, Station 3: **WebQuest**—WebQuest is an inquiry-oriented activity in which most or all of the information used by learners is drawn from the Web. WebQuests are designed to use learners' time well, to focus on using information rather than looking for it, and to support learners' thinking at the levels of analysis, synthesis and evaluation.

11:45 **Break and Shift to Breakout Group Discussions About Technology Presentations**

What was impressive about the demonstrated technologies? What seemed to be their limitations?

Group A1: Oak Room North
Group A2: Sequoia Room
Group C: Spruce Room
Group D: Maple Room

1:00 pm **Break for Lunch**

1:30	**During Lunch, Randy J. Hinrichs,** Group Research Manager, Learning Sciences and Technology at Microsoft Research will report the roadmapping work of the Learning Federation.
2:00	**Improving Middle School Science** *Joseph Krajcik, University of Michigan*

Professor Krajcik will share an overview of challenges to improving middle school science as a contextual foundation for viewing the subsequent technology demonstrations.

Joseph Krajcik is professor of science education in the School of Education at the University of Michigan and a member of the Center for Highly Interactive Computing in Education. His work during the past ten years has focused on working with teachers in science classrooms to bring about sustained change. Working closely with colleagues, he has endeavored to create classrooms that focus on students collaborating to find solutions to important intellectual questions that subsume essential curriculum standards and use new technologies as productivity tools. His goal is to create classroom environments where students are actively doing the intellectual work. He recently published a book with Charlene Czerniak and Carl Berger titled *Teaching Children Science: A Project-based Approach*, intended for use in elementary and middle school methods.

2:30	**General Overview of Each Technology Station** (5 minute limit) *Douglas Kirkpatrick and Marcia Linn, WISE* *Elliot Soloway, University of Michigan* *Kevin Aylesworth, iPaq Probeware*
2:45	**Break and Groups of 20 Shift to View the Technology Stations**
3:00	**Three Stations Showcasing a Variety of Technologies Contributing to Improving Science Pedagogy**

The participants will circulate among three different stations.

- Spruce Room, Station 1: **Web-Based Inquiry Science Environment (WISE)** is a free on-line science learning environment for students in grades 4-12. In WISE, students work on inquiry projects on topics such as genetically modified foods, earthquake prediction, and the deformed frogs mystery. Students learn about and respond to contemporary scientific controversies through designing, debating, and critiquing solutions, all via the Web.

APPENDIX C   121

- Oak Room, Station 3: **Science Laboratory, The Center for Highly Interactive Computing in Education (hi-ce)** focuses on interdisciplinary research on technology and systemic educational reform, especially in the areas of technology and innovative science curriculum projects where thousands of students and teachers in K-12 urban school districts learn science concepts and scientific inquiry processes.
- Maple Room, Station 3: **New Probeware for iPaq Handhelds**, demonstrating how one can use modeling and probeware on handheld computers in chemistry, biology, physics.

4:00	**Break and Shift to Breakout Group Discussions About Technology Presentations**
4:15	**Breakout Group Discussions About Technology Presentations**
	What was impressive about the demonstrated technologies? What seemed to be their limitations?
	Group A1: Oak Room North Group A2: Sequoia Room Group C: Spruce Room Group D: Maple Room
5:30	**Break**
5:45	**Breakout Group Report Back**
5:45-6:00	Group A1
6:00-6:15	Group A2
6:15-6:30	Group B
6:30-7:00	Group C
7:00-7:15	**Concluding Remarks** *Roy Pea and Wm. A. Wulf, ILIT cochairs*
7:15	**Reception and Dinner**

DECEMBER 2001 WORKSHOP PARTICIPANTS

Roy Pea (Cochair), Stanford University
Wm. A. Wulf (Cochair), National Academy of Engineering
Alice Agogino, University of California, Berkeley

David Alexander, Cisco Learning Systems
Barbara Allen, Lemon Grove School District
Sara Armstrong, The George Lucas Educational Foundation
J. Myron Atkin, Stanford University
Mark Atkinson, Teachscape
Kevin Aylesworth, National Research Council
Clarence Bakken, Gunn High School, Palo Alto, California
Stephen Barley, Stanford University
Linda Chaput, Agile Mind
Milton Chen, The George Lucas Educational Foundation
Edward R. Dieterle II, Northwestern High School, College Park, Maryland
Bernard Dodge, San Diego State University
David Dwyer, Apple Computer
Louis Gomez, Northwestern University
Randal Harrington, The Harker School
Randy Hinrichs, Microsoft Research Lab
Terry K. Holmer, National Research Council
Chuck House, Intel
Yasmin Kafai, University of California, Los Angeles
Amy Jo Kim, NAIMA
Douglas Kirkpatrick, University of California, Berkeley
Joseph Krajcik, University of Michigan
Jay B. Labov, National Research Council
Marsha Lamb, Cisco Learning Institute
Tom Landauer, University of Colorado
Edward D. Lazowska, University of Washington
Herbert Lin, National Research Council
Marcia C. Linn, University of California, Berkeley
Charles Lynn, San Antonio Elementary, San Jose, California
Kathleen Luchini, University of Michigan
William Mark, SRI International
Sue Marshall, University of California, Irvine
Miriam Masullo, IBM
Florence McGinn, GKE
Karen Mendalow, Exploratorium
John Mergendoller, Buck Institute for Education
David Messerschmitt, University of California at Berkeley
Jim Minstrell, Talaria Inc.
Eric Muller, Exploratorium
Steve Nelson, Sun Microsystems
Nancy Nien, Alum Rock Union School District, Sunnyvale, California
Nancy Pang, Alum Rock Union School District, Sunnyvale, California

APPENDIX C

James Pellegrino, University of Illinois, Chicago
Harold Pratt, President-elect, National Science Teachers Association
Gail Pritchard, National Research Council
Chris Quintana, University of Michigan
Randall E. Raymond, Detroit Public Schools
Timothy Ready, National Research Council
Jeremy Roschelle, SRI International
Nora Sabelli, SRI International
Bill Sandoval, University of California, Los Angeles
Marlene Scardamalia, University of Toronto
Jane F. Schielack, Texas A&M University
Marshall S. Smith, William and Flora Hewlett Foundation
Jim Spohrer, IBM Almaden
Doug Sprunger, National Research Council
Mark Svorinic, Cisco Learning Systems
Chris Teplovs, University of Toronto
Louis Tornatzky, Tomas Rivera Policy Institute
Uri Treisman, University of Texas at Austin
Michael Turturice, McClintock High School, Tempe, Arizona
Lucia Vega, San Antonio Elementary, San Jose, California
David Vogt, Brainium Technologies
Adam Wieczorek, University of Michigan
Linda S. Wilson, International SEMATECH
Tina Winters, National Research Council

JANUARY 2003 WORKSHOP AGENDA

Planning for Two Transformations in Educational and
Learning Technology

Workshop of the Committee on
Improving Learning with Information Technology (ILIT)

Monday, January 20, 2003

The National Academies
500 Fifth Street, NW, Room 100
Washington, DC

8:00 am   **Continental Breakfast**

8:30-8:45   **Purposes, Outcomes and Introductions**

- Description of previous exploratory planning effort by ILIT committee involving learning researchers, teachers, and industry representatives, using roadmapping techniques
- Commitment of the National Academies to an ongoing role in encouraging the effective use of educational and learning technology

Wm. A. Wulf, National Academy of Engineering
Michael Feuer, National Research Council
Roy Pea, Stanford University

8:45-10:15 The First Transformation: Integrating Cheap, Fast, Robust Computers into Instruction for Every Student in America

- Reducing cost of ownership
- Preparing teachers with adequate professional development
- Providing access to educational software linked to standards
- Involving parents and providing home access
- Who needs to be involved to make it happen
- The impact on learning

Speakers: Barbara Allen, LemonLINK
           Darryl LaGace, LemonLINK
           Steve Rappaport, Advanced Networks and Services
Comments: Cheryl Lemke, Metiri Group
           Wanda Bussey, Teacher Advisory Council
           Geneva Henry, Rice University
Moderator: Edward Dieterle, Harvard University

10:15-10:30 Break

10:30-12:00 Interactive Discussion: What Are the Two Key Enablers of the First Transformation?

Step 1: Breakout groups elaborate possible answers in such areas as:
- Promotion of the vision
- Research demonstrating effectiveness
- Push by industry
- Changes in teacher education and professional development
- Changes in local, state or national education policy
- Funding

Step 2: Participants individually review answers of the different breakout groups and identify their own choices for key enablers

APPENDIX C

Step 3: Discussion of the leading candidates for key enablers
Moderator: Martha Darling

12:00-12:45 **Lunch and Completion of Discussion of First Transformation**

12:45-2:15 **The Second Transformation: Combining Advances in the Science of Learning with IT Capabilities to Dramatically Improve Student Learning**

Research
- Vision for the next generation of educational software and its potential impact on learning
- What research is necessary to develop techniques further and to demonstrate effectiveness

Development
- What development is necessary to scale up these approaches to be used in all schools
- What institutional and financing models are necessary to produce this development

Speakers: Roy Pea, Stanford University
Louis Gomez, Northwestern University
James Pellegrino, University of Illinois at Chicago
Edward Lazowska, University of Washington
Robert Tinker, Concord Consortium
Comments: Nora Sabelli, SRI International
David Vogt, New Media Innovation Center

2:15-2:30 **Break**

2:30-4:00 **Interactive Discussion: Assuming That the Infrastructure of the First Transformation Is in Place, What Are the Two Key Enablers for the Second Transformation?**

Step 1: Breakout groups elaborate possible answers in such areas as:
- Promotion of the vision
- Push by the research community
- Preliminary research demonstrating effectiveness
- Funding for research
- Institutional changes to promote educational software development
- Changes in local, state or national education policy to encourage adoption

Step 2: Participants individually review answers of the different breakout groups and identify their own choices for key enablers

Step 3: Discussion of the leading candidates for key enablers

Moderator: Martha Darling

4:00-5:00 **Comments and Discussion: How Can the National Academies Partner with Teachers, Industry, Learning Researchers, and Policy Groups to Help Bring About These Two Transformations?**

Comments: Milton Goldberg, National Alliance of Business
Marshall Smith, Hewlett Foundation
Terry Rogers, Advanced Network and Services
Moderator: Wm. A. Wulf, National Academy of Engineering

JANUARY 2003 WORKSHOP PARTICIPANTS

Roy Pea (Cochair), Stanford University
Wm. A. Wulf (Cochair), National Academy of Engineering
Jason Adsit, American Association of Colleges for Teacher Education
Barbara Allen, Lemon Grove School District
Bobbie Baird, Texas Instruments
David Barnes, National Council of Teachers of Mathematics
Larry Berger, Wireless Generation
Corey Brady, Texas Instruments
Wanda Bussey, Rufus King High School
Richard A. Chase, Learning Pathways, Inc.
Martha Darling, Education Consultant
Edward R. Dieterle II, Harvard University
Stuart W. Elliott, National Research Council
Michael Feuer, National Research Council
Ann Lee Flynn, National School Boards Association
David Fulker, National Science Digital Library
Milton Goldberg, National Alliance of Business
Louis Gomez, Northwestern University
Sara Hall, State Educational Technology Directors Association
Geneva Henry, Rice University
Michael Hill, National Association of State Boards of Education
Terry K. Holmer, National Research Council
Henry Kelly, Federation of American Scientists
D. Midian Kurland, Scholastic Education

Jay Labov, National Research Council
Darryl LaGace, Lemon Grove School District
Edward D. Lazowska, University of Washington
Cheryl Lemke, Metiri Group
Miriam Masullo, Information Technology Consultant
Steve McClung, Glencoe McGraw-Hill
Ray Myers, U.S. Department of Education
James W. Pellegrino, University of Illinois at Chicago
Louis Pugliese, OnCourse
Steve Rappaport, Advanced Network and Services
Terence W. Rogers, Advanced Network and Services
Nora H. Sabelli, SRI International
Mark Schneiderman, Software & Information Industry Association
Marshall S. Smith, William and Flora Hewlett Foundation
Larry Snowhite, Houghton Mifflin Company
Kendall Starkweather, International Technology Education Association
Timothy Stroud, American Federation of Teachers
Anna Sumner, International Technology Education Association
Robert Tinker, Concord Consortium
Kristan Van Hook, Partnership for 21st Century Skills
David Vogt, New Media Innovation Center
Ken Whang, National Science Foundation
Gerry Wheeler, National Science Teachers Association
Linda Wilson, International SEMATECH

Appendix D

Biographical Sketches of Committee Members

Roy Pea *(Cochair)* is professor of education and the learning sciences at Stanford University and co-director of the Stanford Center for Innovations in Learning. His work is devoted to exploring, defining, and researching new issues in how information technologies can fundamentally support and advance learning and teaching, with particular focus on topics in science, mathematics, and technology education. Particular areas of interest are computer-supported collaborative and on-line community learning, uses of digital video for learning research and teacher education, scientific visualization, and pervasive learning with wireless handheld computers. He was a member of the committee that produced the National Research Council volume, *How People Learn*. He was director of the Center for Technology in Learning at SRI International (1996-2001) and John Evans professor of education and the learning sciences at Northwestern University (1991-1996), where he served as dean of the School of Education and Social Policy. He is a member of the National Academy of Education and a fellow of the American Psychological Society and the World Technology Network. He has a Ph.D. in developmental psychology from the University of Oxford as a Rhodes scholar.

Wm. A. Wulf *(Cochair)* is currently on leave from the University of Virginia to serve as president of the National Academy of Engineering. At the University of Virginia, he is a university professor and holds the AT&T chair in engineering and applied science. During 1988-1990, he was on leave from the University of Virginia to be assistant director of the National Science Foundation (NSF), where he headed the Directorate for Computer and Information Science and Engineering (CISE). While at NSF, Wulf was deeply involved in the development of the High Performance Computing and Communication Initiative and in the formative discussions of the proper government role in developing the National Information Infrastructure. Prior to joining the University of Virginia, he founded Tartan Laboratories and served as its chairman and chief executive officer. The technical basis for Tartan Laboratories was research he conducted while he was professor of computer science at Carnegie Mellon.

Barbara Allen, director of LemonLINK, is responsible for implementing the instructional technology initiatives within the school district, providing leadership for the development of the K-8 instructional technology curriculum and the integration of technology across all curriculum areas. A frequent presenter at major conferences throughout the country, she assists others in integrating technology into instruction and implementing strong staff development components. In December 2002, she was named by *District Administration* magazine as one of the top 25 education technology advocates. Project LemonLINK, a 1997 Technology Innovation Challenge Grant, has received much recognition for innovative approaches to instructional technology, including the ComputerWorld Honors Award (2002), the San Diego Regional Chamber of Commerce Business Roundtable for Education Award—Best Practices (April 2002), the California School Boards Association Golden Bell Award (December 2001), the Ohana Foundation Leadership in Educational Technology Award (July 2000), the National School Board Journal's Magna 2000 Award (April 2000), a Smithsonian award (April 2000), the American Association of Superintendents' Promising Practices Award (March 2000), and *Business Week's* Smart Links Award (May 1999).

Edward R. Dieterle II is a doctoral candidate at the Harvard Graduate School of Education in the Learning and Teaching area. He was a chemistry teacher at Northwestern High School in Hyattsville, Maryland, during the inception of this committee. He had been a teacher at Northwestern since earning his B.A. in chemistry from Virginia Polytechnic Institute and State University. Besides teaching chemistry and advanced placement chemistry, he worked as the school's webmaster and conducted multiple school and countywide staff development sessions on a variety of topics. After earning his M.S. in technology for educators from Johns Hopkins University, he went on to teach multimedia design and technology integration courses for Johns Hopkins University and Trinity College (Washington, DC). He has written and presented extensively for Maryland

Public Television's Teacher Professional Development Institutes and the National Park Service's Bridging the Watershed Program in the areas of effective technology integration and problem-based learning. He is a two-time winner of the ED's Oasis' Master Search. ED's Oasis is part of Classroom Connect, and the national contest recognizes teachers for classroom lessons that successfully integrate technology into instruction. In fall 2002, he began working toward his doctoral degree, and his current research interests include examining and cultivating learning in electronic learning communities.

David Dwyer is the vice president of content development for Apex Learning. Previously, he served as director of education technologies at Apple Computer, Inc. He was charged with developing Apple's 21st century education vision and product strategy. From 1986 to 1996, Dwyer led the Apple Classrooms of Tomorrow (ACOT) project and was Apple's distinguished scientist for education. In that capacity he shaped ACOT's research agenda and built a collaboration with 25 universities that focused on how children learned with computers, on the acquisition of technology skills by teachers, and on innovative uses of emerging technology. The body of work has become a standard in the field. From 1996 to 1999, he was vice president of the education enterprise group at Computer Curriculum Corporation. While there Dwyer developed EdMAP, an award-winning intranet for the unique learning, management, and communication needs of schools. Prior to returning to Apple, he cofounded Edpoint, an education startup aimed at helping parents help their children be more successful in school. Dwyer was also a classroom science teacher for 11 years and was twice recognized as an Outstanding Secondary Educator of America. Dwyer's work is informed by 30 years of experience as an industry leader, researcher, and educator. He holds a Ph.D. in education from Washington University in St. Louis, Missouri, where he specialized in educational change and policy.

Louis M. Gomez is associate professor of learning sciences and professor of computer science at Northwestern University. He is one of the co-directors of the NSF-sponsored Center for Learning Technologies in Urban Schools. The center is a partnership made up Chicago Public Schools, the Detroit Public Schools, the University of Michigan, and Northwestern University. The center is dedicated to collaborative research and development with urban schools that will bring the current state of the art in computing and networking technologies into pervasive use in schools so that they will integrally support science and other curriculum. His primary interest is in working with school communities to create curriculum that supports school reform while connecting schools to broad communities of practice beyond school. Prior to joining the faculty at Northwestern, Gomez was director of Human-Computer Systems Research at Bellcore in Morristown, New Jersey. At Bellcore, he pursued an active research program investigating techniques that improve human use of information retrieval systems and techniques that aid in the acquisition of complex computer-based skills. He has a B.A. in psychology from the State University of New York at Stony Brook and a Ph.D. in cognitive psychology from the University of California at Berkeley.

Amy Jo Kim is vice president for social architecture at There, a web-based gaming company. Prior to her current position, she founded and was creative director of Naima, a company in El Granada, California, that designs cutting-edge on-line environments for web communities. Prior to founding Naima, she was an interface architect with Sun Microsystems. She is a leading specialist in web community design, with a deep and diverse background in client-server engineering, multimedia interface design, and on-line gaming environments. She has a Ph.D. in behavioral neuroscience from the University of Washington.

Edward D. Lazowska holds the Bill and Melinda Gates chair in computer science at the University of Washington. Lazowska received a B.A. from Brown University in 1972 and a Ph.D. from the University of Toronto in 1977. He has been at the University of Washington since that time. His research concerns the design and analysis of distributed and parallel computer systems. He is a member of the National Academy of Engineering and a fellow of the Association for Computing Machinery, the Institute of Electrical and Electronics Engineers, and the American Association for the Advancement of Science. He has served on the 4-person technical advisory board for Microsoft Research since its inception in 1991 and was a member of the NRC Computer Science and Telecommunications Board and a chair of the Computing Research Association and of the Advisory Committee of the NSF Committee for Information Science. He is a leader in the Learning Federation, a group concerned with using information technology to improve learning at the college level, and a trustee of Lakeside School, a coeducational independent school in Seattle.

Miriam Masullo retired from the systems laboratory at the Thomas J. Watson Research Center of IBM and recently ran for Congress. She received M.Phil. and Ph.D. degrees in computer science from the City University of New York. She has 16 years experience in systems analysis and network engineering from the telecommunications industry. For several years, she worked with the American Association for the Advancement of Science on Project 2061. Recently, she has focused on EduPort as a possible model for the education component of the National Information Infrastructure (NII). Masullo organized and conducted the first workshop on the Role of Digital Libraries for K-12 Education. She has worked all over the world, particularly with UNESCO, to influence the development of infrastructure for K-12 education. In 1997, she was named New York City's business educator of the year by the City College of New York Alumni Association and the Rockefeller Group. She recently served at the National Action Council for Minorities in Engineering as director of educational technology and was honored as "a woman who makes a difference" with a technology award at the Women of Color Technology Awards Conference. She is a member of the NRC's Mathematical Sciences Education Board.

James Pellegrino is distinguished professor of cognitive psychology and education at the University of Illinois-Chicago, where he also serves as co-director of the Center for the Study of Learning, Instruction and Teacher Development. Prior to assuming his current positions, he was Frank W. Mayborn professor of cognitive studies at Vanderbilt University and dean of Vanderbilt's Peabody College of Education and Human Development (1992-1998). He also served as co-director of the Learning Technology Center at Peabody (1989-1992). He has a B.A. from Colgate University with a major in psychology and M.A. and Ph.D. degrees in experimental and cognitive psychology from the University of Colorado. His service at the National Research Council has been extensive. He has served as chair of the NRC's Committee on the Evaluation of National and State Assessments of Educational Progress, cochair of the Committee on Learning Research and Educational Practice, and co-chair of the Committee on the Foundations of Assessment. He currently serves as chair of the Panel on Learning and Instruction for the Committee on the Strategic Educational Research Partnership and is a member of the Board on Testing and Assessment.

Louis Pugliese is an experienced education business executive with a long track record of management success at some of the nation's most successful educational technology product and service companies. As chief executive officer of Blackboard Inc., he oversaw the company's operations and long-term strategic direction, shaping a high-growth, diversified business that has gained international recognition as a leader in on-line education. Before joining Blackboard, he served as vice president and chief operating officer of the education division of ETC, a subsidiary of Denver-based Telecommunications Inc. (TCI). Prior to joining ETC, he was director of marketing and sales with Scholastic New Media in New York, and vice president of Turner Educational Services in Atlanta. There, he successfully launched CNN Newsroom and a variety of educational ventures in K-12 and higher education, specifically in Internet and distance education-based content. He is a member of the Education Board for the Software Information Industry Association and the Commission on Technology and Adult Learning. In April 2000, he testified at a hearing before the congressional web-based education committee chaired by Senator Bob Kerrey (R-Nebraska).

Marshall S. Smith is the director of the education program at the William and Flora Hewlett Foundation. Prior to joining the foundation, he was professor of education in the School of Education at Stanford University. Smith was undersecretary and acting deputy secretary of the U.S. Department of Education during the Clinton administration. He trained originally in statistical techniques for research and acquired extensive knowledge of policy issues through his years of government and academic experience. This experience has included key positions in government education policy during the 1970s and 1990s; lead roles as researcher on topics including computer analysis of social science data, early child education, critical thinking, and social inequality; teaching positions at Harvard, Wisconsin, and Stanford Universities; and six years as dean of the School of Education at Stanford. With this broad background, he is able to integrate research on policy questions from several disciplines and to focus on educational process, whether at the level of the individual student in the classroom or at the level of state and national educational reform. He is a member of the National Academy of Education and a fellow at the Center for Advanced Study in the Behavioral Sciences, Stanford. He was chair and principal investigator at the Pew Forum on Educational Reform; member of the National Council on Education Standards and Testing (a congressionally mandated council); and chair of the Subcommittee on Educational Standards. His NRC service includes serving as chair of the Board of International Comparative Studies in Education and as a member of the Commission on Behavioral and Social Sciences and Education. He has an Ed.D. in measurement and statistics from Harvard University (1970).

David Vogt is vice president for technology and chief research officer at the New Media Innovation Center (NewMIC) in Vancouver, British Columbia. NewMIC conducts collaborative, precompetitive R&D in the social dynamics of new media technologies with such companies as Sony, Electronic Arts, IBM, and Nortel. Prior to his current position, he was founder and chief products officer at Brainium Technologies. Brainium is an innovative e-learning company specializing in immersive on-line curriculum content and wireless devices for K-12 markets. He began his career as director of observatories at the University of British Columbia

(UBC) and then as director of western Canada's largest public science center. With the development in 1993 of a virtual science center to support educational outreach, he changed his focus to pioneer human experience in new media environments. He has a Ph.D. in information science, combining computer science, mathematics, archaeology, and astrophysics. He currently also holds the David Robitaille chair in technology applications to math and science education at UBC.

Barbara Watkins is the chief education officer for the Chicago Public Schools. Prior to receiving her doctorate from Loyola University, she was principal of the James McCosh School in Chicago. Her teaching career in Chicago spanned 11 years; during that time she taught all grades K-5 and developed several programs to promote parental involvement. Her leadership style promotes creativity and collaboration among the staff and school community. As a result, several unique programs and school-community partnerships have evolved. She developed the Science Technology Integrated Project, in which Chicago-area universities and schools collaborate to create technology-based science units for children. The project won a Pioneering Partners Foundation Award in 1999. She graduated from Chicago State University with a M.A. in educational administration and later continued her studies at the University of Chicago.

Linda Steele Wilson is the information manager and managing editor for the International Technology Roadmaps for Semiconductors (ITRS). She is also the managing editor for International SEMATECH's 5-year strategic plan. As manager of the roadmap department at International SEMATECH since 1994, her responsibilities include supervising the effort to produce the semiconductor industry's 15-year technology requirements forecast and serving as the publishing manager of the ITRS for the Semiconductor Industry Association. She also serves as recording secretary for the executive International Roadmap Committee for the ITRS and is on the editorial board for that committee. The roadmap efforts became global in 1998; she oversees the internationally held meetings and public conferences that are held annually to develop and present this industry forecast. The global industry roadmapping includes the regions of Europe, Japan, Korea, Taiwan, and the United States. Before joining International SEMATECH, she attained a broad background in the semiconductor industry assignments in manufacturing operations, process engineering and R&D, and research consortium activities, with a focus on failure analysis in chip test and packaging. She graduated from St. Edwards University with a B.A. in English and has worked the last 2 years with George Mason University on the study of industry roadmapping.